A Grain of Wheat

A *biography* by
Margaret R. Decker

Dear Di

As Gail would say
"Go for it"!

Love and God Bless

Rikki + Margaret

New Wine Press

New Wine Press
PO Box 17
Chichester
West Sussex
PO20 6YB
England

ISBN: 1 874367 67 1

Illustrations by Karen Calderwood, 275 Vahland Avenue,
Willetton, Western Australia, 6155
Typeset by CRB Associates, Reepham, Norfolk
Printed in England by Clays Ltd, St Ives plc.

Dedication

To God be all the Glory!
Great and Wonderful things He has done...
Especially in giving us our dearly loved and
courageous brother and son
John Daniel Wickes

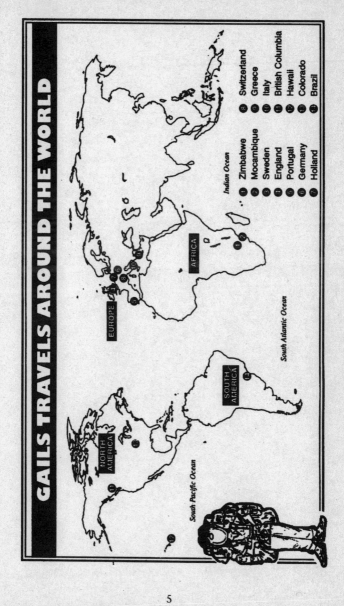

GAILS TRAVELS AROUND THE WORLD

Indian Ocean

1. Zimbabwe
2. Mocambique
3. Sweden
4. England
5. Portugal
6. Germany
7. Holland
8. Switzerland
9. Greece
10. Italy
11. British Columbia
12. Hawaii
13. Colorado
14. Brazil

EUROPE

AFRICA

NORTH AMERICA

SOUTH AMERICA

South Atlantic Ocean

South Pacific Ocean

5

Contents

The title of this book is taken from John 12.24 (New American Standard Version):

> *'Unless a grain of wheat falls into the earth and dies, it remains by itself alone; but if it dies it bears much fruit.'*

All proceeds of this book will go to the Gail Wickes Memorial Fund, Harare, Zimbabwe, for the extension and support of the schools of Casa Ré-om and Kedesh, Youth With A Mission, Beira, Mozambique.

Foreword

He was so young and vibrant, so full of zeal for the cause of Christ. He had every potential to be a great world changer. He was eloquent and yet servant-oriented. His name was Stephen.

What if you were the leader of a man of God and preacher like Stephen? Would you have pulled him from the front lines of service when you had so few workers? Would you have allowed him to be stoned for declaring the truth?

Standing in the background at the stoning of Stephen was another young man who was also zealous. But he was full of hatred and anger at the attention focused on a man named Jesus. This second young man was also eloquent and full of potential. Whatever cause he gave himself to would surely make a difference.

As young Saul of Tarsus looked into the face of Stephen while holding the cloaks of those literally casting the stones, he saw something different. He saw a glow. He saw forgiveness. He saw a face full of love before a crowd filled with hatred.

Saul, who later changed his name to Paul, was

greatly influenced by the death of Stephen. Paul became one of the first missionaries to proclaim the good news of Christ in foreign lands. And through his ministry, millions have come to know Christ and, in turn, to make Him known.

Jesus tells us in Mark 8:34 that we must take up our cross and follow him. Jesus had to literally carry His cross. Taking up our cross, in a spiritual sense, involves different things for each of us. But it will always involve death. Death to our own desires, our flesh, our will and our determination. And sometimes it involves literally laying down our lives.

When a young person dies we naturally feel that their death was untimely – their life cut short.

But when a seed is planted in the ground, it must first die before it brings forth life. Only through the death of the seed can life and fruit come forth. The fruit from the seed speaks of multiplication. In the same way, Christ's death on the cross brought forth multiplication. Likewise, when a follower of Jesus loses their life, whether in a moment of recreation, joy, service, or sorrow, that life is multiplied in Christ to add to the multitude that no one can count on the final day.

As believers, we are tempted to feel that the Body of Christ has been robbed when a young person dies. We think of their joy, their love, their faith, their obedience, and service and so much potential. Yet, their death is not without purpose. God's strategy is always above human comprehension. And from the perspective of a wise, heavenly father, a day is as a thousand years and a thousand years as a day. He sees that the days of some who have walked this earth, though few in number, can be multiplied to a thousand years worth of impact on a sinful world.

Why did Gail Wickes have to die? Why was her life seemingly cut short? I don't know the answer to that question. We cannot always fully explain the hard questions of life for, as Paul tells us, we *'see through a glass darkly.'*

But this one thing we know. Gail is present with the Lord. She is now part of the *'great cloud of witnesses'* we read of in Hebrews 12. We all have friends and loved ones among that crowd. And we miss them.

The book in your hand recounts the life, the love, the service, the joy and the sorrows that were known by one of these witnesses, Gail Wickes. It tells of her experiences of serving Christ in Mozambique, where pioneering a missionary work was a great challenge. She reached out to children who were lonely, needy, hungry, naked, homeless. She was an ambassador of Jesus Christ to them. I drove across Mozambique to visit Gail's YWAM team. We were told to drive fast because war was raging around us, and guerilla fighters would often shoot at cars attempting the journey on one of the only roads kept open. As I looked into the faces of Gail and her co-workers, I could hardly begin to comprehend their anxieties, fears, struggles ... and dedication. As I think of those I have influenced for Christ, it seems like only a small amount compared to those, like Gail, who have paid a higher price.

Gail is one of my heroes of the faith, and she's also a hero in the hearts of many of her friends and missionary co-workers. She was a witness. And she still is a witness. She's a grain of wheat that fell to the ground and died ... but she will not abide alone.

Loren Cunningham
Founder and Chairman
Youth With A Mission International

Prologue

As I have sorted through Gail's diaries, letters, study notebooks and photographs, which have provided much of the material for this book, I have laughed, cried, and been deeply humbled, over and over again. I have discovered facets of our daughter which had been hidden. She had an amazing capacity for studying the Bible, and a deep love for her Heavenly Father, desiring to know and serve Him above all else.

She also deeply loved and appreciated her family, and delighted in her many friends scattered around the world. Her enjoyment of all of God's creation, flowers and forests, mountains and valleys, sea and sand, sunsets and sunrises, only increased with time, as did her commitment to the people of Mozambique, especially the rejected, neglected children.

People have said they remember Gail most for her smile, that she was always laughing, and often in the middle of riotous fun. She had a great sense of humour, but underneath there was a strength of character and singleness of purpose. She never accepted that mountains could not be climbed, moved, or made into molehills.

Thank you, Gaily Girl, for being so special.

Thank you to my dear husband Rikki, for his constant encouragement, and without whose patience in finding my 'lost' chapters on the computer, you would not be reading this book!

To our daughters Lindsay and Carol – thank you for your interest and support, and to all those who have contributed in any way, may God repay you for your love and faithfulness.

To all who contributed to the richness of Gail's life, thank you so much.

A very special thank you to Gail's friend Karen Calderwood for her illustrations.

Thank you Lord, for telling me to 'Write Gail's Story.' I do pray you will enjoy it, as much as I have enjoyed writing it, but more than that, I hope it will challenge and inspire you to do great exploits for the King of kings. Gail did so much – please catch her vision and help Jesus reap a harvest for His Kingdom, while there is still time.

Margaret Decker

Your Love broke thru'!!!

O my God
I long to love You.
I long to express my love for You
so that people
will see,
and hear,
and understand,
and know
You are love.

Your love is here to be shared
in a smile,
or a hug;
in flowers,
honest words;
even in tears,
heavy hearts;
in sharing honest emotions
and small,
special,
thoughts....

Chapter 1

Beginnings

C-R-A-S-H! Glass shattering, metal buckling, the car turned over in seeming slow motion. Then the awful, awful silence. The dust settled, the cicadas returned to their tuneless trilling, and a tiny shocked baby began to cry.

On 29th August 1964, Richard John Decker, a science graduate from the University College of Rhodesia and Nyasaland (now University of Zimbabwe), married Elspeth May Elderkin, a primary school teacher. Elspeth had a gift for music and attended the Methodist Church. Richard, better known as Rikki, his Scout nickname from Rudyard Kipling's mongoose Rikki-tiki-tavi, was teaching Chemistry at his old school, Churchill. In his spare time he practised his hobby as a magician, especially enjoying entertaining children – an interest which began when he was eight years old.

While Rikki was writing his MSc, thesis, a daughter, Gail Lesley was born, on 3rd October, 1965.

Rikki and Elspeth, planning a holiday at the Victoria Falls before Christmas accepted an invitation to take part in a Christmas programme, in a small rural town, en route, on 18th December. After Rikki's magical entertainment they resumed their journey.

Many roads in those days consisted of just two tarmac strips with deep dust and hard corrugated soil on either side. Negotiating a single strip while being overtaken, or avoiding on-coming traffic, was fraught with danger, with the ever present possibility of a flying stone shattering a windscreen. Thick sand caused Rikki to lose control and as the car began to turn over, Gail was thrown clear from Elspeth's arms, Elspeth fell out of the opening door and the car rolled over her. At 25 years old, Rikki was suddenly a widower with a two-month-old daughter to care for.

After Elspeth's funeral, Gail's maternal grandmother insisted Gail be christened. During the service Rikki realised he had little to offer a growing baby, and sincerely gave her back to God. Probably one of the most significant things he ever did for his daughter.

Sitting alone each night after Gail was asleep, Rikki would relive the horror of the accident. He felt he had caused the death of his beautiful young wife – one relative actually called him a murderer – and many did not think he was capable of looking after Gail. This made him cling all the more to his daughter and his independence.

One day he did contemplate suicide, but at the very moment he was considering this, Gary Strong, a Methodist minister from the nearby church, knocked on the door and said God had prompted him to call round at that particular time.

From this lowest point Rikki rekindled his desire to get a DSc, the highest academic qualification available to him. Rikki's parents were living on a smallholding some miles from town, and he began spending weekends with them, building a wooden GP14 sailing yacht he had planned for some time.

During 1966 Rikki was awarded a research fellowship at the University which changed his routine considerably. Once Gail was asleep in the evening, he would put her in a carry cot, drive to his laboratory, deposit her on the end of the bench and work through the night. He would return home in time for her early morning feed, and busy himself with her needs and household chores, sleeping whenever she slept during the day.

A young wife in the same block of flats expected one child, and delivered twins. She would often pop in to ask for advice, particularly on how Rikki got his nappies so white! On a number of occasions Rikki was aware of feeling Elspeth close by, sharing in his play time with Gail – a happy experience, but not one to be sought after.

The following year Rikki was appointed a junior lecturer and needed to spend more normal working hours at the University. He moved to a larger flat in an adjoining block, by piling things into and onto his twin-tub washing machine. His new neighbours, Roland and Jeanette, had two children slightly older than Gail. Jeanette had been at Teacher Training College with Elspeth, and volunteered to care for Gail during the day. This arrangement lasted happily for 18 months. Meanwhile Gail began to realise her family was different – she had a Daddy, but her friends had a Mummy and a Daddy, and Rikki asked God for a mother for Gail.

Rikki had always been shy, and since the death of his wife had become a virtual recluse, although he did, somewhat reluctantly, accept an invitation to a private party at the University. Among the guests was

Margaret, who had a keen interest in sailing. Rikki never dreamt that night he would meet not only a mother for Gail, but a crew ... for life!

We were engaged in January 1968, and married on 25th May the same year. Gail was just over two-and-a-half years old.

Chapter 2

Growing Together

'Hallo Daddy, Hallo Mummy.'

Blue eyes under touselled fair hair peered round the bedroom door, soon followed by a gappy grin – Gail had fallen against a stone step and broken her top four front teeth not long after they had grown through – and this was the first morning we were all together in our new home, a three-bedroom brick under tile bungalow on one-and-a-quarter acres, three miles from the University. When we asked Gail what she would specially like to have waiting for her in her new home she said 'a kitten,' and six-week-old Fluffy – a somewhat unfluffy grey tortoise-shell **male** – we were told – came to live with us, miraculously surviving for 20 human years, and producing one kitten when **she** was nine months old!

The first six months were somewhat traumatic. I made two major mistakes; the first was reading Dr Spock's child care book chapter on two-to-three-year-olds and how easy it was to psychologically damage them. The second was trying to copy Rikki's handling of Gail rather than being myself. She naturally ran to him for everything to begin with, but we all adjusted slowly, and laughed when one day Gail prefaced a comment with the words 'When me and Daddy married you...' I felt secure at last.

In January of 1969 we flew to England for Rikki's PhD oral examination at Imperial College, London. After this we drove to Scotland where Gail was introduced to sea and sand in the lovely University town of St Andrews. It was a wet and windy day but it did not put her off – in fact the sea held a special fascination for her all her life.

On returning home 'Julie' came to live with us. She was Gail's imaginary friend who sat with us at every meal, and came with us wherever we went. Gail was terribly upset one day when getting into the back seat of the car, the door was closed, leaving Julie standing outside.

On 7th December, 1969, Lindsay Margaret was born. As soon as she arrived home from the hospital, Gail sat on her stool as close to the pram as possible and proceeded to 'read' her favourite book to her sister out loud.

In the new year Gail started Nursery School. We were concerned that she might react badly to school so soon after Lindsay had joined the family, but we need not have worried. She was quiet and shy but an able student. Once she arrived at school wearing odd socks, sandals on the wrong feet, and a jersey buttoned askew, but was very proud that she had dressed herself.

One day while helping to dress Lindsay, Gail asked, 'How do you know what to do with a baby when you haven't had one before?' Having prayed about answering Gail's questions adequately, I shot up a 'Help' prayer now, reminding her how Mummies got together to talk over tea sometimes, and how the

Nurses at the Clinic helped when we took Lindsay for her checkups and vaccinations. Then I continued, 'If anyone ever says I'm not your real Mummy, it's true, but you can tell them you're special because you have two mummies; one in heaven, and one to look after you here, because Daddy chose me specially to look after you.' 'Oh' said Gail, 'is she a star?' 'I don't see why she shouldn't be a star' I replied, and Gail accepted this happily and never mentioned it again.

Almost two years later, in August 1971, we climbed on a train which took three days to reach Cape Town, and boarded a Union Castle Mail Ship bound for Southampton, England. Our final destination was Dortmund, Germany, where Rikki had a Von Humboldt Scholarship for eight months at the Institute for Spectrochemistry and Applied Spectroscopy. The first two months involved full-time language

study for him at a Goethe Institute in Iserlohn, 30 miles away, so we bought a car, and learned to find our way around within three days of arrival.

We were able to enrol Gail in the local British Army school and her report said 'Gail is extremely conscientious in all her work. She is much less confident than her ability would cause one to expect and any difficulty tends to take on the aspect of a major crisis. She likes to know exactly what is expected of her and works best in an ordered and well directed atmosphere. She is shy in making friends, but is very loyal to her close friends. Gail is particularly able in Reading and Writing. Her creative writing is imaginative and fluent. She reads with expression. She seems totally unaware of her own abilities. She presents a challenge in keeping her supplied with suitably interesting and demanding books. Written work: Beautifully neat.' Praise indeed, considering Gail at six years old had overcome the difficulties of being left handed. She took a particular interest in the caged mice in the classroom and was upset when they escaped.

Carol Ruth was born at 9.15 pm on 10th November in Dortmund's Knappshaft Krankenhuis. Because of Rikki's language studies, we prayed the baby would arrive either on a weekend or Wednesday – his half-day. She arrived on a Wednesday with the outside temperature 13 degrees below freezing. Gail was thrilled with her new sister and could hardly wait to share her news in class next day.

We returned to Zimbabwe when Carol was six months old. On arriving home the first thing Gail did was sit all her dolls and toys on her bed in orderly rows and tell them where she had been, and what she had been doing. An indication of the teacher she

26

would become in the far future perhaps? God seems to slip these milestones into our lives once in a while, but we only recognise them when we look back over the distance of years.

Chapter 3

Growing Up

'Well done, Gaily girl!' Bursting with pride, we cheered loudly. Gail had just come first in a 40-metre flat race in the school sports.

Prime Minister Ian Smith's Unilateral Declaration of Independence was six years old, and the war of resistance between the Rhodesian armed forces and 'freedom fighters' increasing in intensity. Rikki, along with most able-bodied young men, faced the dangers of military duty 'in the bush' one month out of every two. He hated leaving us, but we adjusted, and carried on with 'business as usual'. Of course, there was great excitement whenever Daddy came home.

The year Gail turned eight she won a School Junior Essay silver floating trophy cup, and a miniature cup that she could keep. Lindsay was in Grade One by this time and Gail never minded having her sister tagging along. Her end of year report said 'Gail has been a joy to teach. She is very conscientious and gives of her best at all times. She is co-operative and enjoys all class activities in a quiet, mature manner. She has maintained a high standard of work throughout the year and her examination results were excellent.'

She was also a joy to have at home. She loved her sisters and there was very little friction between them. She never talked much, but was content, and happiest wearing shorts and climbing to the top of the tallest cyprus tree, especially when it swayed in the wind. She enjoyed tennis, swimming and netball, and was healthy apart from the usual childhood diseases which the three girls passed on to each other on the very last day of each incubation period. We were in quarantine for weeks on end.

In Grade Six, aged 10, she progressed to Poetry, winning a first prize with this poem:

Birds in Flight

He swoops over the barren hillside
His wing's spread out wide
His beady eyes scan the ground
Looking for a mouse.

A fierce hawk
A bird of prey
Flying through the bright blue sky
Sailing over the great mountain
He spots a mouse.

Down he swoops like a thunderbolt
He clasps the mouse in crooked claws
Then sails into the heavens
And turns a short sharp turn
To his nest.

As he turns, his brown breast shows
The mottled brown feathers
He dives down low
And swoops up high
And returns to his nest.

In her final year of Junior School, Gail played first team hockey and netball, enjoyed Scripture Union camp, Brownies and church youth group, and was happy that she and her sisters were all in the same school for one year. She ended the year with A and B Grades, and a growing awareness of her Christian faith operating on a day-to-day basis.

We discovered Youth With A Mission – YWAM – about this time, during their first Discipleship Training School in the country. The family was invited to a Love Feast, and it was then Gail first heard of the work YWAM was doing.

Gail started learning the guitar and before long it became an extension of herself. 'New Creation', the name of a band Gail and some friends formed, inspired by the Amy Grant's and Don Francisco's of this world, had more enthusiasm than expertise singing 'Old Man's Rubble' and after their first church appearance someone suggested 'Perhaps you should try singing lessons.'

In the September of Gail's first year in High School we went to Dortmund, Germany, again. This time all the girls did school work at home. Rikki brushed up his very rusty Latin to help Gail, and we all enjoyed examining things under her microscope.

This was a particularly lonely period for Gail as she worked diligently with her school books every weekday morning and having no friends of her own age. Not far into the Sabbatical I woke in the early hours to hear Gail sobbing. She said she felt she was an ugly person because she had no friends. These became precious times over mugs of hot chocolate, talking and praying together, while the world around slept peacefully. Within a few days Gail met Susie, a German girl her own age, and her long-haired terrier dog Flokka, living in the next street. Susie's English was very good, and she and Gail were soon spending a lot of time together. God answered our prayers.

Each weekend we went sightseeing, and as with our first visit to Germany, we lived as 'German' as we could, enjoying local food, and absorbing the traditions of Rikki's forebears, especially at Christmas and Easter.

On a never-to-be-forgotten trip to the River Rhine, we had food poisoning on the journey home. What should have been a one hour drive took four or five, as a little voice from the back seat would request yet another stop.

We planned some skiing in Northern Italy where luxury accommodation was lent to us by some very special German friends. A few hours out of Dortmund on a very wet and windy Saturday afternoon, our car was hit from behind by a long-distance truck driver. Thankfully no one was hurt, but Gail's diary says 'It was horrible.'

We reported the accident at an autobahn police station, and continued to Darmstadt, south of Frankfurt. We had a hazy recollection of hearing about Basilea Schlink's Sister's of Mary and needing somewhere to stay for the night, Rikki found a public telephone. With a quick prayer he opened the enormously thick telephone directory and the first name his eyes focused on was 'The Little Sisters of Mary'. They invited us to their 'Land of Canaan', and when we told the girls we were going to visit a convent, their faces dropped. By the time we left on the Sunday evening, none of us wanted to go! Gail's diary read, 'It was 1st April, and none of us had remembered.'

The following morning our car was considered a write-off, and we were able to sell it, and claim on the Insurance. Because the damage was entirely the fault of the other driver, we were told to hire a car – newer and more powerful than ours – which enabled us to drive beautiful mountain roads we would not have used in our car. Sometimes the snow was banked

2 metres high either side of the road. We enjoyed the skiing, returning to Germany through Switzerland. People questioned why we were taking our family back to war-torn Rhodesia. For us, we were going home.

We were invited to an out-of-town wedding and the family was waiting in the car, when it was discovered Gail was wearing her newest T-shirt, emblazoned with a large, colourful transfer of her favourite singing group 'ABBA'. I did not consider this suitable wedding attire, the only occasion I can remember having a serious disagreement with Gail. She eventually changed into something I thought more suitable but was very upset for most of the journey. To my chagrin, and Gail's delight, every person in a singing group taking part in the service was wearing a colourful T-shirt!

1980, the year Rhodesia became independent Zimbabwe, two books, *They Speak with Other Tongues*, and *Nine O'Clock in the Morning*, began a radical change in our lives which ended with a personal encounter with the Holy Spirit. With our new praise languages came a new boldness and power to live our lives for God. In the Bible, Acts chapter two, verses one to four give you the details of the first time this happened in the New Testament church.

Not long after this we had a family holiday in a National Parks cottage on the banks of the Zambezi River, several kilometres above the famous Victoria Falls. Gail seemed especially quiet for a day or two, and finally, one evening when Lindsay and Carol were in bed, she shyly asked if we would pray for her to be filled with the Holy Spirit. We did so gladly, and she immediately began praising God in a new language.

As the announcement that Robert Mugabe had won

the Presidential election was made over the intercom system in the school, Gail lost her closest friend. Everyone was making quite a noise, and it was only when things had quietened down a bit that Gail realised something was very wrong with Tracy. She had suffered a fatal epileptic fit – the only one she ever had. Gail insisted on playing a basketball match that afternoon and would not let the team down. Although shocked, she had peace, knowing that Tracy as a Christian, was safely with her Lord. Her sudden death had an effect throughout the school, and her funeral service challenged people to consider where they would be spending eternity – in heaven or in hell.

High School presented no problems to Gail. She played basketball, and in her second year became a very good squash player. She enjoyed leading the singing for the Christian Union, and started a guitar club. Later she led the Christian Union, taking responsibility for school assembly each Wednesday morning. She joined the Library Club, acted in at least one school play and helped produce others, she was a tent leader on several Scripture Union camps and enjoyed travelling to 'Youth Week' in South Africa with friends. Photographs show Gail and her friend Viv covered in mud from head to toe – there was a mud hole just for this purpose. A wonderful international opportunity to flex spiritual as well as physical muscles. Occasionally Gail was gated for coming home late. It was never intentional – she just forgot time when having fun with her friends.

One weekend the couple whose wedding caused the ABBA incident came to stay. Together we went to our local swimming pool, and the three girls lay on their towels in the sun, talking and laughing together, while the rest of us sat at a table under a poolside umbrella. The husband sat watching the girls for a long time, and finally shook his head and said 'That's amazing.' We asked him what he meant, and he said 'Do they always do that?' 'What?' Our eyes swivelled to where our family sprawled on the grass. 'Do they always get on so well together? I've never come across that in a family before.' We felt glad and sad at the same time. Glad that we had such a loving family, and sad to think it was not the norm for many families, as God would desire it to be.

We joined our nearest church, and were soon involved in the Sunday School, either as pupils or teachers. At a church fellowship evening, one of Gail's admirers tried to kiss her in the dark garden, and was kicked hard on the shins for his efforts. Rikki became an Elder and in 1981 the church asked us, as a family, to establish a sister church in a neighbouring suburb. We started meeting in a double garage, and as Gail was keen to acquire a new steel string guitar, Rikki bargained to pay her $2 each time she played for services.

At the end of her Form Four Ordinary level examinations, we talked much about Gail's future, investigating many different professions and University courses. By the time she wrote her Advance level examinations two years later, she had set her heart on becoming a Speech Therapist.

Where am I going?
Who am I?
Why am I running?
Am I trying to hide?
Why the emptiness?
Why the fear?
Its good to know He's near

Sometimes people,
Even friends let you down
Sometimes you feel alone
Even when you're with the crowd.
When its raining.
And the sky is grey
Its good to know He's the way

And Jesus said I Am
In Me you are complete
I'll show you the way
In me the truth you'll see
I give you life abundantly

Feeling bugged 'coz I let myself be bugged

I wonder
    why I need you
    why you need me (if you do)
    why people need other people
    why relationships are such
            a large part
                    of our lives

I wonder
    why the emptiness
    why the lonliness
    why the frustrations, anger, pain
    why the desire to commune,
            to share, to love
                    with you

Maybe the nature of the Creator
        has been molded
            into the creation
Maybe.

Criticism......

                it slices like a knife
        thru putty,
            to reach the bone,
        and expose it as
                weak, immature,
                    not up to standard.
And everytime a word falls
        out of a mouth,
            to be swallowed by an
                open ear,
    or when a thought is invited
            to stay for a while & entertain;
            the blade is thrust deeper

        and a slice of goodness & stength
            & commitment, falls away
            and is lost in the dust.
And soon there is none left.
    and the bone appears as it was made to be,
            weak, immature, not up to standard;
        stripped of its goodness, & strength
        & commitment.
        Alone, unlovely. unloved.

38

Chapter 4

The Future

'Three M level passes in Maths. What am I going to do now?' To study Speech Therapy Gail needed an Advance level pass in mathematics, and she had missed again. It seemed, after all the form filling, interviews, exams, and expectations Gail's world had come crashing down. She cried bitterly, and wanted to run away from everything that was familiar. She had so set her heart on going to Cape Town or Johannesburg, in South Africa, to train in the profession she believed God had called her to.

The previous year Gail and a friend had done computer aptitude tests in which Gail did quite well. It was now too late in the year to apply for any other university course and Gail was invited to join the staff of the computer company to train as a programmer. This gave her something to do immediately, and time to reconsider her options. After careful thought she agreed.

This began another difficult time for Gail. Rikki was asked to join the same computer company and became Gail's boss! Initially people avoided talking to the Boss's daughter. She tackled the work with her

usual dogged determination, and became a very professional and accurate programmer. When she left, two years later, she had written some significant systems for the company.

Gail began saving for a car, and prayed specifically for a Mini with a stripe down the side. Several possibilities were not seriously considered as none of them had a stripe. Eventually, she heard of a red countryman with two blue stripes running from front to back, and she knew it was hers.

Now that she had wheels, Gail dragged her friends to various Christian activities, and joined a drama group which she had always considered 'not her ministry'. She loved it, and soon afterwards started clowning as well.

She tried learning Shona, spoken extensively in Zimbabwe and understood in neighbouring countries. It is not an easy language and Gail did not study long enough to become proficient. She attended several Praise and Worship seminars, did a Bible School Course by correspondence, and prayed for specific Russian Christians imprisoned for their beliefs.

Gail was corresponding copiously with friends – by this time scattered around the world. In a letter to Dorothy in South Africa she wrote of her options and said 'I'd really love to go to YWAM or something.'

In 1986 the family had a holiday in South Africa, and just after returning home Gail wrote in her diary that she had given up hope of YWAM or Bible College – and that she felt she was drifting with no direction.

Soon after this a visiting preacher at Greystone Park Fellowship spoke from Proverbs 4:23:

'Above all else, guard your heart, for it is the well-spring of life.'

and Psalm 37:3–5

'Trust in the Lord and do good; dwell in the land and enjoy safe pasture. **Delight yourself in the Lord and He will give you the desires of your heart**. *Commit your way to the Lord; trust in him and he will do this.'*

Gail wrote:

'My desire of my heart is to go to YWAM. I believe it is a God-given desire. Therefore God will give it to me!'

This was a significant turning point in Gail's life. In one short service, God gave her the direction she was needing, and the confirmation of what He had started in her years before. From this time she was totally motivated and nothing was going to stop her.

Our home was a hive of activity the week before 14th June in preparation for a 'Farewell High Tea', dress to be 'Formal 1920s' and croquet on the lawn! Gail, and her friend Karen, more commonly known as 'Soggie' because she loved soaking in the bath, combined to celebrate their Twenty-First birthdays a few months early, before travelling overseas together.

It was a lovely afternoon, and the originality of the outfits amazing. Guests signed their names with fabric paint pens on two lace-trimmed table cloths to commemorate the occasion. To finish we shared a simple communion service, singing together with Gail and her guitar, and praying Gail and Karen would travel with God's blessing, guidance and protection.

GOD,
I love being creative like this.
I love to express myself,
to   let all the thoughts running
        around in my mind
          out in the open,
      So that I can see
      and share with You
          who I am,
    and what is happening
          in my life.

        Maybe God
    I'll be able to share
      a bit of myself
      with other people,
      So that they can
  discover life with me.

      Thank you for feelings.
  Thank-you that I can feel happy,
      or sad, or sorry,
          or pain,
        or release.
          I am alive
      Because You live in me.
          Thank you !!

Chapter 5

Launching Out

'Help!' 'Phew, we made it!' Gail's diary entry for 20th June reads – 'Mad panic to get to the airport on time – still packing hand luggage when we should have already left. Lots of forms to be filled in as well – don't know what I would have done without the folks help!!' Fortunately she did take a couple of seconds to scribble a rough itinerary for us – Karen's folks didn't even get that. At the airport there was a crowd of people to make sure they did leave, and among the teasing and laughter, a good few tears as well. Gail contained herself until she was in the plane, and had a good cry after reading the goodbye cards.

Their first impression of Athens was concrete, concrete, and more concrete as well as being very dry and dusty, and on arriving at the domestic terminal, they found their flight to the Island of Skiathos, had been cancelled. Propping themselves against a wall for 6 hours, looking like a couple of '3rd World Groupies' they were thankful no one knew them. When they finally boarded the 'funny little biscuit tin' aeroplane they were rewarded with a fantastic view of Greece from the air, and the sea

seemed as clear as holiday brochures always show it to be.

It was hot and humid in Skiathos and their back-packs were heavy on unaccustomed shoulders. Waiting for a bus, Gail hated every moment and wanted to go home. The bus was crowded and her pack kept tripping people up. They missed their stop, and ended up at the last beach on the bus route. Getting off, lost and scared, they both wanted to go home. A 'little Greek chappie' directed them over a hill to Banana Beach where they could sleep, which at first seemed a good idea. They found out later it was the nudist beach, so were glad they had decided against it. They were sitting under a tree, realising what a hysterical situation they were in, and agreeing to get the next bus back when a taxi driver took pity on them and drove them to where they should have got off in the first place. A tall, blond girl squealed at them from the balcony of a flat across the road. Greatly relieved to have found school friends Karen and Janice, and Karen's sister Vanessa, their holiday was about to begin. The prayer for safety had already been answered, the first of many times.

The girls shared a huge flat with a fantastic view of the sea, and on a clear day the mainland mountains, and Gail and Karen began to relax and enjoy themselves. Gail especially loved the shades of green in the trees, the wild flowers, the goats, donkeys, horses and mules. They lived right on the road which went around the island, and if one was rich enough there were little motor bikes for hire. As the girls were not in this category they enjoyed walking everywhere.

The sea was lovely to swim in with fantastic seaweed and fish to watch, but by lunchtime it was too hot to stay on the beach. On their second day another 'Greek chappie' arrived from the Taverna across the road with a bottle of Greek Retsina, the paint stripping national wine made from gum-tree resin. While Karen was taking the label off the bottle to stick in her diary the visitor made a pass at her. Her eyes nearly fell out with surprise, and he immediately became persona non grata. Moussaka eaten on a vine shaded taverna verandah, was a treat for Karen and Gail as their staple diet during their travels consisted of packet soups and muesli from home.

One day arriving back at the flat after a storm, they found the electricity was off, the flat flooded, and their newly washed underwear scattered over the neighbouring vineyard. The electricity was reconnected next day, by which time the water was off. The joys of living in foreign lands.

Another day they discovered 'ice blinks', natural yoghurt with honey and peaches, which were fine until the honey ran out. Vanessa's birthday was celebrated at Vromilimnos Taverna. On hearing 'happy birthday' people at the next table ordered a big cream and cherry pudding with a sparkler on top for them. After that the Greek music and dancing started.

Karen and Gail took a boat trip to the Islands of Lalaria and Kastra. They found Lalaria beach covered with beautiful multi-coloured pebbles, and Kastra with three churches like the one in the monastery on Skiathos. A lovely day out, ending with a final trip to the beach for a swim, photographs, and supper at a Taverna.

When it was time for Janice, Karen and Vanessa to return to England, all five girls took the bus into Skiathos. Karen and Gail discovered their flight to Athens had been cancelled, but found a little Greek lady who spoke zero English happy to accommodate them for a night.

A walk through Skiathos town after dark was beautiful. Most of the shops were open and it reminded Gail of Christmas in Germany with everyone in festive mood – a really magical atmosphere – with people selling nuts and jewellery on the pavements and artists painting Grecian scenes. It made Gail feel homesick – she so wanted to share the 'magic' with people at home.

Ten days away from home and it was time to move on. The flight to Athens gave them a good view from the air again. The following day they climbed to the Acropolis, couldn't afford the entrance fee, so climbed the hill behind it instead. A man seemed to be following them, so they attached themselves to a French couple on the walk down. While sitting in Sintagma Square two young Greeks offered to show them around. They accepted, and were conducted round the National Gardens including the zoo, changing guard outside Parliament – Gail thought the huge pompons on their shoes highly amusing. Then to watch a rehearsal of a Greek Comedy from above the Stadium, and on to sit on 'Holy Hill' next to the Acropolis to watch it illuminated by a light and sound show. Then back through little restaurant-lined streets, amidst lots of Greeks dancing.

The title in Gail's diary for this day was 'Living under the shadow of His wings...'

Next day they got into Ancient Agora as students with their Youth Hostel cards, stuffing themselves with cherries and watermelons. They met up with 'Mike' and 'George' of the day before and took a half-hour bus ride to an up-market suburb on the coast – an amazing contrast to Athens – with huge shopping complexes, flats and gardens.

Karen's alarm clock woke everyone in the Youth Hostel dormitory at 5 am next morning so the two girls could get the 6 am airport bus, destination – Italy.

On arrival they met an Australian girl, an experienced backpacker, and decided to stick together. The road to Rome was lined with fields full of grass bales and flowers. They met three German girls, and trailed around together in the midday heat, trying to find accommodation they could afford. They eventually settled in a campsite 20 kilometres outside the city.

The usual sightseeing followed – Colosseum, Venice Palace, Monument to the Unknown Soldier, the Pantheon, Trevi Fountain and the Quirinale Piazza. Returning to the campsite Gail had a good time with God and felt homesick again.

They had an early start to reach the Vatican before 10.30 next morning to catch a glimpse of the Pope. Gail wanted to cry, but didn't know if it was because of the magnificence of the Cathedral or because there were so many tourists wandering around who were only there to look at a fancy building. Gail was especially upset by an old man behind her during the service doing a lot of 'grabbing'. Every time she moved, so did he, and there was nothing else she could do in such a huge crowd. Gail's back was giving trouble, and by the time she had stood on the bus back to the station, with someone behind her doing even more 'grabbing', she got off in tears. It was a relief to get back to camp.

They saw the Sistine Chapel next day, as well as the Vatican museum with impressive Raphael tapestries, and brilliant paintings. The rest of the day was spent relaxing at the camp site, and quite a party developed late into the night. Next day Alitalia flew them to Pisa and they took a train through fields of yellow sunflowers, and vineyards, to Florence. Karen prayed for Gail's back and she had no further trouble with it after that.

They enjoyed the famous Uffizi Gallery, and while praying in one of the little chapels of the Cathedral

Gail wondered what God thought of such ornate churches. She decided God looked at heart attitude rather than surroundings.

Early next morning they missed the bus into Florence, and the train as well. They managed to arrive in Pisa in time for the flight to Milan and then to Como by train. Or at least it should have been to Como but they found they were heading for Venice instead. A girl in the compartment spoke some English and showed them how to get back to Milan.

Arriving eventually at Como, they bumped into a young American Christian – the first they had met among their fellow travellers. The Youth Hostel was really lovely, small and friendly. They had a huge meal and afterwards walked round the lake to see if they could find the frog on the North door of a church – patting its head was supposed to bring good luck.

Lake Como was beautiful. At night the lights reflected in the lake, and twinkled up into the mountains, and some of the old town buildings were softly illuminated. Walking in the peace and beauty after the busy cities was a welcome relief, but soon they were travelling again, towards Venice.

They broke their journey in Milan, admiring the beautiful stained glass windows and Leonardo da Vinci's famous painting of the 'Last Supper' in the church of S. Maria del a Grazzia. Gail was horrified at the L.4000 admission fee, and was sad that the painting was not in better condition. She thought the figures so lifelike one almost expected them to speak.

Venice looked weird from the air, and much smaller than expected. Gail and Karen scrambled for a place in a crowded Youth Hostel and went looking for a meal. It cost L.25850, and they realised why the guide books warned against eating out in Venice! They loved the Venetian glassware and other tourist attractions and realised too soon their holiday had ended. Their final destination – London, England.

The flight over the Alps was clear, and they arrived to a special London welcome of blue skies and warm sunshine. Karen and Gail soon learnt the art of travel in England, racing frantically up and down stairs to get to the right train platform, and officially joined 'the Sewer Rats of London', negotiating the tube train system.

Gail and Karen had planned to join the crowds in London, for the wedding of Prince Andrew to Sarah Ferguson, but were pleased to avoid the people and the rain and watch everything on television instead. They did go to Buckingham Palace to watch the couple leave on honeymoon, and then queued for an hour-and-a-half in the cold, outside Westminster Abbey, to see the beautiful flowers. Gail decided she would like flowers like that at her wedding!

Karen quickly found secretarial work, but Gail discovered computer programmers were not required in London. After several anxious weeks, Gail arranged to stay with Terry and Joan Parsons, parents of her good friend Helen, in Welwyn Garden City, and work in St Albans. If Gail was out for the evening, her first words on getting back were always 'Do you want tea or coffee?'

Gail's friend Nibby wanted to get to Cape Town, South Africa, but did not have all the money for her fare. Gail volunteered to buy her bicycle for two hundred pounds, and then felt totally irresponsible spending so much money, but when she rode the bike she fell in love with it. 'Bee-line' conveyed Gail safely along the miles between Welwyn Garden City and St Albans almost daily.

She loved the countryside in all conditions, autumn colours, winter frost and snow, and budding spring – even when it was pouring with rain. She wasn't so keen on riding home in the dark as the winter days got shorter, and she hated passing squashed hedge-hogs on the country lanes.

A thoroughly enjoyable trip to the Lake District and Scotland was organised with several friends. As always, Gail revelled in the beauty of the countryside – the more remote and rugged the better.

Trips to London to meet friends, and to stay week-ends, were arranged as often as possible. Friends were always very important to Gail.

One of Gail's friends, Pam, considered Gail quite daft. She bought Pam a flying pig, which caused much hilarity. Gail said she felt 'a bit of a nerd' buying Pam the pig, but she enjoyed doing it. Pam especially appreciated Gail's faithfulness – once she said she would do something she always did it.

Gail wrote a song to Pam:

You opened up your heart
    all I saw was pain
I looked into your eyes
    you were hiding in the shadows
I don't know how to tell you
The words are heavy on my heart
But please don't mistake
    my silence for indifference.

Your brokenness – it tears my heart
    I feel it bleeding.
You have given me so much
    but my emptiness can't heal you.

I have to wipe away the tears
Coz I can't make you smile
But perhaps you'll catch a glimpse
    of how I long for Him to touch you.

Only God could have given
    such a precious friend
I see your face reflect
    the image of His son.
And I know He longs to hold you
And comfort you in His arms
He longs to heal the hurt and dry your eyes
    He longs to see you smile.

Gail joined a YWAM outreach to the flotsam and
jetsam of the world living in the Earls Court area of
London. This provided the first experience of a
culture totally foreign to her – the deviants, addicts
and prostitutes. It also fanned the YWAM flame in
her, and she started searching for God's future plan,
and actively saving towards her Discipleship Training
School, the initial course all YWAMers are required to
complete. God promises that when we begin searching, we will find, and before long, Gail found she was
heading for Sweden.

Before this, however, Gail joined an Oakhall skiing
trip to Austria, confirming that skiing was the sport to
top all other sports, and making a whole bunch of
new Christian friends. One, Grace, came to Zimbabwe
for a holiday the following year.

Karen decided to return home to Zimbabwe. It was a
sad parting of the ways, as they had seen and done a
great deal together, but Ecclesiastes chapter 3 says
'There is a time for everything,' and it was time for both
of them to move on.

Thank you for laughter God.
Thank you for that special sparkle
                    in a friends eyes.
Thank you for the fun & joy there is
                    in being friends;
In knowing that you are loved
         and accepted and enjoyed,
By someone who is special to you.

What an incredible gift -
         the gift of friendship & laughter
And also of sadness,
              of sharing,
                   of hurts;
Of understanding - or trying to understand
         what is happening on the inside,
And trying to identify with that
         and to share it.

God - you are the one who
         makes ordinary people into special friends,
              and who brings joy and laughter.
And God - thank-you for being my friend;
         the greatest friend
                    I could ever know.

Chapter 6

YWAM Sweden DTS: Discipleship Training School

'God, these next five months are yours!'

29th March 1987 was a beautiful day as Gail ran round the lakes near the Parsons home for the last time, praying excitedly about the new phase of her life which was about to begin – the YWAM Discipleship Training School in Restenäs, Sweden. True to form, she thought her train left at 14.40 and just before leaving the house discovered it left at 14.10. So friends Pam and Jackie missed seeing her off. Gail watched the receding coastline of England from the deck of the ferry – it was the end of a happy chapter in her life. The trip to Sweden was a bit daunting. There were no cabins available, she was surrounded by people speaking Swedish, and she was seasick every time she ate anything.

Next morning she answered many questions at Gothenburg customs because there had been no time to get a visa in England. Eventually she got a three month residence stamp in her passport. Sweden was really pretty, and Gail enjoyed the hour long drive to Restenäs, on the coast. She soon adjusted to goat's cheese and porridge for breakfast, and found the base far bigger than expected. Everything was still in the frozen grip of winter, but the little rocky outcrops on campus reminded her of Africa, which helped her feel more at home.

The Discipleship Training School began with introductions, schedules, rules and job assignments. Gail was put in the laundry – and thought this hilarious. One thing she disliked was washing and ironing. Her Swedish companion in the laundry spoke very little English, but wanted to learn more, and they managed to communicate quite well with an English/Swedish dictionary and lots of sign language. There were piles of sheets to be put through a wringer which constantly jammed, and the whole machine would stop. Fortunately for the sheets, Gail was soon moved from laundry to kitchen duty. Other duties included washing dishes, floors and toilets. She enjoyed cleaning the gymnasium most because while doing it she could sing at the top of her voice.

She got to know her fellow students by playing volley ball, sharing coffee breaks, walking to the nearest shops in Ljungskile for chocolate bars, and joining anyone who was eating, playing silly games, talking, singing, or just having fun.

On 6th April lectures began, each teaching day starting with aerobics at 6 am. Lectures in Swedish were translated into English for the benefit of the foreign students. Gail's small group was a mini league of nations. She hated their first meeting and felt upset afterwards as everyone else seemed to think it had been great. Early next morning she ran towards the sea and, sitting on the foot bridge to Restenäs island in the early morning mist and squawking sea gulls, talked to God about it. The small group that day was better, as people shared about their families. American Doug and Hans from Holland believed Gail's Dad would go into full-time ministry. (Thank you, you guys – you were absolutely right, but that is another story.) Gail found over and over during her DTS all the loving, caring, sharing, growing, laughing, crying, listening, learning were such special experiences, surrounded by God's love and the support of her new friends.

Gail and two friends travelled to Gothenburg for Easter. Standing on top of the biggest rock at the harbour, Gail watched the setting sun, the sea stretched out vast and beautiful. She enjoyed the buskers in the town centre, and the openness of the people listening to a Christian group singing and preaching. She was fascinated with the young Swedish girls traditionally dressed in head scarves, long dresses, red cheeks and 'freckles' on Easter Saturday, and flags flying from garden flag poles celebrating Easter Sunday.

Steffan, who spent time in Zimbabwe, took the girls on a tour of Gothenburg, including a fishing boat in the harbour, and the fish market, and drove them all the way back to Restenäs.

The following week Gail was given a prophecy – that she was fluent and able to communicate things to people where others had failed. She would be a counsellor – speak wisdom – restore relationships, organising some sort of mission in the world. She would start with one, that would grow to many groups. She was not to be afraid of a small beginning. She was a fruitful tree – she was not to be afraid to use her gifts – the fruit would be good and sweet.

At the end of the teaching segment of the DTS, outreach teams were planned for Malawi, Yugoslavia, and Northern Ireland. This was challenging, and Gail found it hard to know where God wanted her to go. Finally, after much prayer alone, and with others, she decided in the early hours of the morning to go on outreach to Malawi, and went to sleep greatly relieved and at peace.

Meanwhile the foundations for an outreach to Gottenburg were being laid, with prayer walks in the Nordstrom shopping centre, on Friday evenings between 6 pm and midnight. Gail was distracted by french fries in MacDonalds during one of these evenings!

2nd May – Masquerade day. The night before was spent working on costumes. Not only was it dress-up time, but eat-up time too, with national dishes from all the countries of the world represented on the school. Gail was not sure she liked such differing foods combined together, but photographs show it was a lot of fun.

Book reports and lectures continued to keep the students busy, when they were not trying to find shortcuts to the nearest ice cream shop, practising other people's alphabets, learning songs in new languages, roasting hot dogs, eating popcorn, or attending local church services. Gail took every opportunity to be outside in God's beautiful world, going for 'walkie talkie' times with God as often as she could; she loved being outside so much she would go for a run whatever the weather. She played football against a junior high school, enjoying the practice in the gym hall when it was too wet to play outside. She thought it was good fun playing inside because you could kick the ball off the walls. The YWAM team won!

'Lidagin Whopsy Day' fell on 23rd May. Gail and friends invited the whole DTS to celebrate this fictitious character; the history of Lidagin was explained – born 1818 – died 1880 – he mined gold in Sacramento, California, and was renowned for re-inventing the lid, so it could be used to pan gold. Guests were asked to come in fancy dress, and enjoyed a treasure hunt, lots of singing, some Jewish dancing, and **food**. It was a nightmare to prepare but Gail was in her element.

On 28th May, Lars Wideberg who had been teaching on intercession and spiritual warfare joined Gail's outreach team to pray with them, giving Gail the same prophecy about wisdom, and an ability to communicate in other languages. This was really encouraging, and she began considering a YWAM Mercy Ministry School, in Sweden, the following September. The six-month training would be three months of teaching, and three months of practical skills like plumbing, car maintenance, and basic first aid so necessary for modern missionaries. This school required a commitment to work somewhere in missions for at least a year afterwards. One thing she lacked was the finance.

Her diary writing stopped at this point, possibly for two reasons. One was busyness towards the end of school, and another, the sudden death of one of the students, which upset everyone deeply.

At the beginning of June the Malawi outreach team began rehearsing their drama *Agape*. Gail said it took eight hours to learn and they were so stiff at the end of this, they could hardly move. It was beauti-fully produced and costumed, with simple scenery allowing them to travel easily and perform it anywhere. It showed how Jesus took on Himself the sin of the world, and no one saw this drama without being profoundly challenged.

Gail was one of two 'support leaders' for the outreach, a job for which she felt totally inadequate. It made her trust God more, and learn to listen to what He was saying for the team. It involved helping the team leader as much as possible and sharing the responsibility of the day-to-day needs of the team.

28th June, 1987, 10 crumpled, tired but excited YWAMers arrived at Harare International Airport, lugging bulging rucksacks, bed-rolls and guitars with them. Gail introduced us to team leader Elisabeth from Germany, Anna, Ulla, Anneli and Pia from Sweden, Hans and Annerieke from Holland, and Doug from America. It was a great team which we came to love in the week they stayed with us in Harare. They performed *Agape* several times in schools and churches. One morning the team was driving through central Harare, dressed for a school performance, when they stopped for a red traffic light. Gail's role was 'the devil' and a poor pedestrian glancing at her driving the car, disappeared across the road as fast as his feet could carry him!

After a week of rest and acclimatization, it was time to pack again, the girls leaving their shorts and jeans behind as they would not be allowed to wear them in Malawi.

They flew to Blantyre, boarding a bus at six next morning to drive for five hours to Nsanje in the south of Malawi. Pastor Gomwa their interpreter, gave them useful and much needed insight into the customs and culture of the people, which averted a lot of

embarrassment and misunderstanding. They pitched their tents close to Pastor Jack's house. The shower was a makeshift grass enclosure, and the 'kitchen' was under the eaves of a thatched mud hut. Cooking on open fires, water had to be fetched from the river. Cattle, goats, pigs and people all used the same water supply. The far side of the river was Mozambique, and because they were living so close to the border the police had to be informed of their movements at all times.

The village nestled under beautiful Nsanje mountain. Gail was responsible for preparing and cooking the food, helped by the rest of the team. On different occasions they were given a couple of chickens, and two goats, but after having them killed and chopping them up, Gail almost preferred the staple diet of bananas and rice.

Pastor Jack made a room available in his house as a lounge which gave the team a welcome break from their tents. Being white skinned, they only had to stick their noses outside their tents and they would have a huge crowd of smiling black faces peering at them from a distance of 20 cm! An incredible way to live, but a wonderful opportunity for evangelism. The people were ready to listen to the team because they got involved, living with them, eating the same food, the girls carrying buckets of water from the river on their heads in the traditional way, buying food in the market, and playing with their children.

The heat was intense. Each day would start with a worship service at 7.00 am, followed by teaching at 9.00 am, children's, young women or young men's meetings at 3.00 pm and a main meeting at 6.00 pm. African time is different to any other, and one has to sing for quite a while before the people have gathered for a proper start. Gail always disliked women's meetings, but was involved in running three, having total responsibility for one. She said it had to be God, because she actually enjoyed it, especially the last one which was held in a refugee camp. The team spent four days preparing for one final ministry day at Ngabo, before it was time to pack up and catch the train for a 13 hour journey back to Blantyre.

Everyone enjoyed the luxury of Limbe Sports Club's showers, toilets, and food. God graciously allowed them to reach civilisation before the entire team succumbed to malaria or diarrhoea and vomiting in varying degrees. Annerieke was hospitalised with bad malaria, and flew back to Harare, while the rest of the team travelled to Zomba to spend time with Pastor Gomwa's own church.

The team snatched a little sight-seeing time, driving up Zomba plateau to enjoy vast and magnificent views. At the end of the drama at Tali, they were mobbed as people grabbed for Christian literature.

Their final drama performance was at Blantyre Christian Centre, before returning to Harare for two days, still suffering from malaria and stomach upsets, but glad to be reunited with a much improved Annerieke. They were not fully recovered before it was time to fly back to Sweden for report back, heralding the official end of the Discipleship Training School. On arrival by ferry, at Malmo, the team was grateful they were met by two YWAM vehicles and they were deeply touched when given fresh roses in welcome.

The team which went to Ireland lived in luxury, saw no violence, worked with churches and did a lot of street drama and evangelistic barbecues. They had a lot of fun and were very united, considering the diverse personalities on the team. The team that went to Yugoslavia had a tough time – there was little opportunity to do drama, and they had to have a Yugoslav national responsible for them the whole time they were in the country. When it came time for the Malawi team report, they delighted everyone by dressing in African skirts, singing a song in Chichewa and dancing African style. To the embarrassment of their team leader they also did a skit of how she used to give everything away!

English Sue, American Olivia and Gail took a final walk to the bridge to Restenäs Island. When they first arrived at Restenäs the three used to go to the bridge and wonder what they had done to themselves by going on a DTS. Just before they left for outreach they went to the bridge to pontificate on all they had learnt and how much they loved Restenäs and the DTS. On this, their final walk, at one in the morning, they were amazed to realise how they, their plans and ideas had changed. God had changed them.

Gail and Anna went to Lyseberg, a huge amusement park in Gothenburg, where Gail fulfilled a long held ambition to loop the loop on a roller coaster. Her stomach had not fully recovered from the Malawi trip, and she was sick after each ride, until Anna, tired of this, prayed for Gail. She wasn't sick again. Anna won 'Gideon' (pronounced Yee-dee-on in Swedish) a 75 cm. fluffy blue and white striped worm with a bell on the end of his tail, and gave him to Gail. He hangs in our home still.

Gail enjoyed spending one Sunday on a Communications Team visiting churches in Stockholm, sharing about YWAM, what had happened on outreach, and generally encouraging people to get into missions. She loved the city, often called 'The Venice of the North' but found it greener, cleaner and prettier than the Italian namesake. She welcomed every opportunity to visit Swedish families in their homes, and wished she could speak Swedish properly in order to communicate more easily.

Gail travelled to England on the ferry with Anna, especially enjoying sharing a cabin with two other Christian girls. They did all the usual things in London, especially those which cost nothing, like seeing St Paul's Cathedral lit up at night, and running up the down escalators and down the up escalators in the underground train stations, until Gail tripped on the way up a down escalator, and fell hard on her knee. It was agony for days. She was still taking antibiotics to heal some infected mosquito bites – a legacy from Malawi.

She and Anna missed the boat-train connection from London to the ferry at Harwich, as they started their return journey to Sweden. They had to re-route, and just as their train was leaving, Gail's friend Pam raced along the platform and thrust Thirty Pounds into her hand. By the time they arrived at Anna's home in Orebro, Sweden, they had One Pound left between them. Gail wrote – God always provides just what we need.

O Jesus I want to love
        Show me how
                in practical ways.
Let people know
        You are love
                Because they see
                    Your love
                        in me.
Don't let me be afraid
        of what they might think,
            or that they might
                        misunderstand,
            or get the wrong idea.
I   don't want to be a dam
        with a wall
I want to be a
                    fountain,
                        a   spring
                            a waterfall.
Let Your love flow thru me
        to a   hurting
                    world.
            I trust You, Lord

66

If you have eyes to see
  or a little boy next to you
or if you have someone to call your friend
if you felt the warm sunlight in your face
  today
or saw the blue sky & laughed
you must know what it means to sing
  God is so good.
If you know what it feels like to laugh
  with God
to have fallen flat on your face
& have Him reach out
& say I still love you, take my hand;
to feel Him lift your guilt,
  to ease your pain,
  to have Him sooth your tired,
    worn, broken heart.

then you must understand how good He is?

Oh, i wish for hours & hours of gentle spirits
& easy laughter.
clear eyes & warm handshakes
forgiving hearts & unselfish pocketbooks.

hours & hours of little touches of brilliance
    in everyday history:
    Mary & her perfume,
        paul & a song in jail
            Jesus spending the afternoon
                with zacchaeus
    or washing the tired feet of His followers
        or simply holding a child
            on His lap.

Chapter 7

YWAM Sweden MMS: Mercy Ministry School

'Hej, Hej, hemskt mycket hej! Mina Kara Familjie' (Hello, hello, very much hello! My dear family).

'I'm back in sunny Sweden, except it's not sunny any more, it's raining, but that doesn't matter does it?'

Matthew 6.8 says '...*your Father knows what you need before you ask him,*' and Gail's heavenly Father had once more provided all that she needed and she was back in Restenäs ready for the Mercy Ministry School.

There were six students on the school and by the end of the first week Gail knew the course was going to be excellent, lots of hard work, but more relaxed than the DTS. Students were allowed to prepare their own breakfast and supper and they were free to re-arrange their furniture. One of the many projects was to study the country they planned to work in – difficult for Gail because she was not sure where that would be.

By mid-October she was revelling in the beauty of

the autumn colours, and picking blueberries in the forest. Assignments, book reports and visiting friends often crowded out things like sleep and correspondence, but the family kept contact by telephone.

In early November, Gail's ex-boss from England, Gail and some friends prayed for God's protection as they took a short holiday break. Through unfamiliar Stockholm they had several near misses, and later were protected from a serious accident when a car overtook oncoming traffic on a hill.

The course fascinated and challenged Gail every day. She loved learning about foreign cultures and realised how much more knowledge she needed to effectively reach people with the love of Jesus.

Personality profiles were part of the teaching on how to get on with fellow missionaries, and gave Gail some interesting personal insights. Her analysis claimed she was introverted as opposed to extrovert – but growing more and more extrovert, intuitive as opposed to sensory, feeling as opposed to thinking and perceptive as opposed to decisive. Her personality summary said: 'Full of enthusiasm and loyalties, but you seldom talk of these until people know you well. You care about learning, ideas, language, and independent projects of your own. You tend to undertake too much, then somehow get it done. You are friendly, but often too absorbed in what is going on to be sociable. Little concerned with possessions or physical surroundings.' There was Gail, in a nutshell.

Amid commitment to study and learning, Gail still enjoyed every opportunity to visit Swedish friends and one weekend was volunteered to dress up as a clown to hand out invitations to a church coffee bar – a new project – and at least two people became Christians, which was an exciting beginning.

On 13th December, the longest night of the year, Sweden celebrated 'Lucia' – a very special festival, and Gail was thrilled to be there for it. Lucia was a Christian who was martyred around 300AD. Traditionally each year, a young girl with blonde hair, wearing a long white dress and red sash, parades with four lighted candles on her head-dress, followed by other girls dressed in white, carrying candles, and young men dressed in white with pointed caps, or in red suits, singing songs and 'chasing the darkness

away'. The YWAM base invited neighbours and guests to their Lucia parade.

This was followed by 'Antshillvania' a children's musical production they had been working on for several weeks. The children were 'ants' dressed in black tops and bright shorts or skirts, and wore antennae made from polystyrene balls on pipe cleaners and elastic. Some of the balls were a bit heavy, so half the children had antennae hanging down, or at right angles to their heads, but they looked cute anyway.

Everyone enjoyed it, and the following Lucia feast of fruit, nuts, toffee and traditional saffron bread snacks.

Gail had been corresponding with Angus Hulley, from her home church, while he studied for a year at Christ for the Nations in Dallas, Texas, and God organised a string of miracles which enabled Gail to fly to Amsterdam to meet him as he returned to Zimbabwe at the end of his studies. It was freezing cold but they managed some sightseeing, and lots of talking over cups of strong Dutch coffee.

Gail spent a totally white Christmas with Anna and her family in their holiday cottage in the far north of Sweden. She loved the little red and yellow painted houses, half buried in the snow, surrounded by forests of pine and silver birch, and a completely frozen river. The temperature dropped to −20°C but when the temperatures hovered around zero it was a good time to make snowballs and snowmen because the snow stuck together. Gail helped make a snowman called Gubby – a 'proper' snowman made from rolling big balls of snow. She didn't know it could be done for real, but thought they were only depicted like that in cartoon books!

She was ecstatic when she caught a glimpse of the Northern Lights one night. It wasn't a colourful spectacular, but in the middle of the night, with no moon, or big town nearby, the sky showed a weird light. It was so strange – really awesome in a way, and she wondered if Jesus was coming back, but decided she hadn't heard the trumpet, so it had to be the Northern Lights. She wanted so much to see them before leaving Sweden, she asked God, and was thrilled with yet another experience of His love for her.

Gail helped chop down a Christmas Tree in the forest, although it wasn't that simple. She had a real problem walking in the snow, feeling like a three-year-old because she kept falling down, as they wandered through snowdrifts to pick the perfect tree. The tree, decorations, candles and woven baskets full of little plants they dug out of the snowdrifts were prepared on 23rd December. Christmas Eve began with rice porridge for breakfast, then everyone opened one present; the rest remained under the tree until after dinner at 10 pm. Gail felt sorry for the children having to wait so long.

Traditional Swedish Christmas food includes pork, herring fish called sill, and lutfish, a sun-dried, lime-cured ling, a relative of the cod, which takes several weeks to prepare. On Christmas Day everyone was up at 6 am for church, which Gail loved, even though only two of the carols were familiar to her.

By 8th January 1988 Gail was back in Restenäs, waiting to get a cheap youth flight to Portugal. The base leaders decided she should fly to avoid the costly and slow process of acquiring all the visas she needed to travel overland. The base was quiet as the other students had already started the overland journey, and the staff were on holiday for a few days. Gail grabbed the opportunity to use the computer, relax a bit, and write some letters.

Portugal was very cold and wet – the kind of weather that 'got right inside you and wouldn't go away.' Everything remained damp, especially the washing. Gail found her shoes leaked or fell apart completely, because of the muddy conditions, and her white socks became chocolate coloured with mud stains. God understood, and prompted someone to give her enough money to buy some new shoes.

She found Portugal strange, with poor and rich living closely together. The area the team was working in was poor, with the highest crime rate in Lisbon, but with the most beautiful, naughty children who stole Gail's heart. They worked closely with the permanent YWAM team in Lisbon who helped them in many ways, especially with translation.

The guys on Gail's team were building a house for an Angolan refugee family living in a shack. The walls were finished, when the hired van was broken into and almost all the tools were stolen – most of them the personal property of one of the team. Essential replacements had to be bought, and a few more were borrowed. Satan's attack was sudden and the team really felt the struggle, but they fought back and won. They prayed for another van because the one they were using was brand new, and the hire charge was half the cost of building the whole house. That same day they got the use of an older van, much better for transporting building materials, and more in keeping with the area in which they were working.

While some of the team worked on the building, the rest held outreach services, doing drama in schools, and Gail worked with the children. She was sad to realise the children had little idea of discipline or respect, and badly needed some kind of authority in their lives. It was hard working with them, but six of them gave their lives to Jesus, and others showed real interest, and the team could see a change in them. This team also visited new Christians and gave some Discipleship teaching.

Ulla, Gail and Isabel, their Mozambican translator, visited one of the girls who always sat in the front at church, giggling and generally disturbing the congregation. They thought she was in her mid-teens and somewhat immature, but discovered Zezee was 22, had been married at 15, and had three children of 6, 4 and 2 years. She had a nervous breakdown, and while being treated was baptised into the Mormon Church. Her husband was now living with another girl who had born him a child, and would not allow Zezee to visit her own children living with him. This scenario seemed to be quite normal for the area, and Gail found it heartbreaking.

Gail and Ulla were responsible for some of the shopping and organising the kitchen for the team. One day between domestic duties, some children showed them a wild, beautiful park nearby. They played games with them there and told them stories, but sensed a heavy atmosphere until they discovered it was a place for prostitution. There was a military base on the other side of the park and children as young as 12 years old went there to earn money!

With these kinds of spiritual forces against them, the team spent much time in prayer and fasting, asking God to move powerfully in each situation.

Post from home arrived spasmodically, but one day Gail learned that her father would be in Britain on business in February. This gave her direction for the immediate future, as the second half of the Mercy Ministry School had been cancelled. Only two students had enough money to continue, and it was not economical to run the course for so few people. By booking before 29th February, Gail got the cheapest ferry ticket available from Sweden to England, and her life changed yet again.

Love

Out of sight ... out of mind?
A bit of distance relieves the pressure
        gives room for the imagination
                to roam
        to wander where it pleases
                into dreams of the future
where everything is open and shut
                and clear cut
and not dependent on emotions
        or feelings or circumstances
        or 'helpful, encouraging friends',
where everything falls into place
                and is covered by love
                and romantic mists
        and dancing sunbeams that
                chase away the shadows
        that could be forming in
                the corners of my heart;
But you will return
                and your visits will
                        jolt me into reality,
where you're not my dream

but you're real, living,
   eating, breathing,
      thinking, feeling,
   leaving me torn between
my imagination and my
      common sense
my heart and my mind
my God, my job, my purpose
      and you...
            you and me
         me and you!

                  (sigh)

   or   you
                  and
                              ?
                        me.

Chapter 8

Mozambique

'I'm committed to Mozambique for a year, but I think I will be there for two. I won't learn Portuguese in less time than that.'

After returning to England, and seeing her Dad, Gail worked in several computer jobs, and a Chinese Take-away, to earn enough money to join Anna and her church on a skiing trip to Austria, and pay for her ticket home.

She felt a bit irresponsible spending money on another skiing trip, but decided to go, wondering how many more opportunities she would have.

She wrote another poem:

Decision Time

My head is spinning round and round
My heart is churning – I'm upside down
I don't know what's right
I don't know what's wrong
I haven't a clue what's going on

And I need a bit of direction
I know I need to hear God's voice
I need to find the security
Of knowing I've made the right choice

My mind's in a muddle, I'm a bit confused
One way I win, one way I lose
If I walk down one path the Lord will bless
But if I take the other, I'll never rest

And I need a bit of direction . . .

God said He'd put His Spirit inside
The Spirit of truth, to lead and guide
I need to find the road engraved on His heart
I'll trust the Spirit to show me where to start.
And I know I'll find my direction
If I listen I will hear God's voice
In Him I'll find security
'Coz together we'll make the right choice!

Meanwhile, she stayed again with Joan and Terry Parsons in Welwyn Garden City, often spending weekends with friends in London, enjoying services at Holy Trinity, Brompton, and praying about her future. She fulfilled a lifelong desire to pick armfuls of bluebells in all their spring glory, amongst the trees and open spaces of the English countryside, shortly before she flew back to Zimbabwe.

She arrived in Harare two years and a day after she had originally left, and her friend Karen was with the family at the airport to welcome her home. What a full two years it had been. Gail's friendship with Angus progressed over the next three months, but a few days before she left for Beira, Mozambique, to see what YWAM was doing there, they realised God had given them different visions for the future, and these did not include them married to each other. They were deeply saddened by this, but remained good friends and continued to pray for one another in their different ministries.

Gail wrote the following song, 'for Gus':

So many different people
From different walks of life
Different songs, different dreams
Different pain and strife.
But deep within us there's a cord
That's stronger than I know
It goes deeper than I can understand
It's His love that makes it grow . . .

And I'm so grateful to God for you.
I'm so thankful for all we've shared
When I've needed a friend
And I turn around
I've always found you there.
I'm so grateful to God for you.

One day our paths crossed
It must have been part of His plan.
And we've walked down the road together
Like children, hand in hand.
And even if our paths now go different ways
And we don't know where they lead
I know we're headed for the same goal
And someday we will meet . . .

And I'm so grateful.

The day Gail left for Mozambique, 17th November, 1988, God shone as it were a spotlight on a portion of my Bible reading for that day – Isaiah 54:1–5:

' "Sing, O barren woman,
*   you who never bore a child;*
burst into song, shout for joy,
*   you who were never in labour;*

because more are the children of the desolate woman
than of her who has a husband," says the Lord.

"Enlarge the place of your tent,
stretch your tent curtains wide, do not hold back;
lengthen your cords,
strengthen your stakes.
For you will spread out to the right and to the left;
your descendants will dispossess nations
and settle in their desolate cities.

"Do not be afraid; you will not suffer shame.
Do not fear disgrace; you will not be humiliated.
You will forget the shame of your youth,
and remember no more the reproach of your
widowhood.
For your Maker is your husband –
the Lord Almighty is his name –
the Holy One of Israel is your Redeemer;
he is called the God of all the earth."'

Interestingly, years later, Gail said God had given her the same verses. In fact God repeated those verses to the team in Beira many times over the years, until they became 'founding verses' for the work which was later to be established in Beira.

Not long after getting to Beira, Gail wrote a Song of Praise:

Gracious Father, precious Jesus
I want to glorify Your name.
You are faithful, You are wonderful
You are always the same.
Never changing
Always constant
Your love surrounding me

Your Spirit always leading
  to where I ought to be.
Such security in knowing You
The rock that does not move
My fortress, my hiding place, my God.

Gail joined Anneke, a nurse from Holland who was leading the team, New Zealand nurse Dellanie, American midwife Laura, British nurse Debbie, Brazilians Marta and Helena, Fiona from Australia, and Engela from South Africa.

They were living in a small flat on the inland side of Beira and initially Gail made herself useful to the

team by doing the housework, washing, ironing (!) and cooking. She had to fetch water in buckets from the tap downstairs in the dusty yard, whenever the water was turned on, maybe once, or on good days, twice a day. She began studying Portuguese, and, according to report she was a good student. She managed, as always, to be in the middle of anything that caused hilarity, which helped to break the stress the others worked with each day in the clinics and hospitals. So many people living in one flat with a single bathroom meant keeping to a strict roster and time quota, and the team prayed that when they moved it would be to somewhere with more extensive bathroom facilities.

Saturday was 'beach day' although it was not always easy to get there, with bicycle chains which broke, or pedals which fell off, but it was a great way to meet the local people, always ready to help. Beach time was also a good time to meet some of the other missionaries working in Beira.

It took Gail a while to adjust to a quieter social life than she had been used to in Harare, and to the temperatures and humidity at sea level, but she revelled in life in Mozambique, and knew she was where God wanted her to be. She slipped easily into caring for and keeping contact with children in the orphanage at Dondo, outside Beira on the main road to Zimbabwe, regularly taking them food and clothing, and playing games with them.

In 1988 Mozambique was still in the midst of a 'liberation' war which had been long and bitter. The 'safe' roads were treacherous with enormous potholes, and often attacked by rebel forces, and one was only allowed to travel during the hours of day light. It was not even safe to be out on the streets of Beira after dark. The team had most of their supplies sent from Zimbabwe because there was very little to buy in the few shops that were open. Fruit and vegetables were scarce, and seasonal, and Gail learned to make home-made bread, and eat fish, which she eventually came to quite enjoy.

The kitchen was always a good place to chat, and Gail and Dellanie used to do this a great deal. They became close friends with Gail bouncing her views about love and acceptance of the Mozambicans off Dellanie, and expressing her desire to serve them.

Once the rains began in Beira the mosquitos arrived in full force, as did the mud. The sewers of Beira had not been maintained, and the street drainage systems long broken, so one avoided walking through puddles as far as possible. Special people Nick and Vic Fereira, living in what was commonly known as the 'Manica Palace' were wonderful friends to the girls, always offering hospitality and support, and available to help with problems when they arose.

Gail soon discovered a family of 6 orphans living in the flat next door. The oldest was a girl of 14. The five-year-old sister, called 'Miseria' – misery – and her mates used to steal Gail's buckets when she went to fetch water, and it often turned into a game, chasing them down the road.

She began teaching English at the Samora Machel Secondary School to students 16 years and older. Never having taught before, Gail had to rely heavily on God for wisdom, as well as on primary readers obtained in Zimbabwe. She provided most of the pens and paper for her students too, as the school could not afford to supply them. She wondered why her students kept asking her how many children she had, and if she was married, in that order. This puzzle was eventually solved when she discovered that many of her pupils were married and had children!

Gail's knowledge of Portuguese increased rapidly in the classroom situation but one day she said something in the staff room, and all the teachers roared with laughter. She wondered what awful faux pas she had made, but was quickly reassured that what she had said was quite correct, it was just amusing to hear her speaking in the idiom her teenage students used.

On the beach, watching the tide come in, getting her skirt wet as the waves caught her, Gail would think of all the people in her church in Harare. How they showed God's love to her in their support, prayers and love, and how much she needed and appreciated them. It encouraged her to know they were there, and she used to ask God to repay them a hundred-fold.

Gail loved people – Noemia, her Portuguese teacher; the Catholic priest who had been in Mozambique for 30 years, and translated the New Testament into an African dialect, but who did not know Jesus as his Saviour; a physics teacher who would not go to church because evolution was taught in school. Over the years contacts like these were multiplied many times, but Gail never knew if she had any impact on their lives, if they ever met her Jesus in a personal way, but she always prayed that they would. Gail once said to Anneke, the team leader, 'I want to understand the way the Mozambicans think. That will help me to work with them.' She would get upset when Mozambicans came to visit, and the other YWAM girls would not sit with them the whole afternoon. She felt this wasn't right, and that they needed to adjust to the culture, even if it meant sitting together for hours saying nothing.

Some of the kids in school were great, some were not, and the rest tended to blur into the masses. Gail had seven classes of between 41–45 pupils in each, and her voice took strain with talking at a raised volume for six hours a day, and even louder on occasion in order to enforce discipline. The first time she asked her classes to write essays, she anticipated having to spend the whole weekend marking them, and was overjoyed to find most essays were only five lines long.

She felt a little insecure when a pupil joined one of her classes who spoke better English than she spoke Portuguese. The whole class tried to copy his work, giving up the little thinking they used to do for themselves, but God gave her the wisdom she needed and she soon gained more control. She became a respected teacher, known for her love and discipline, and enthusiastic support when one of her classes played a football match, or some pupils needed extra coaching. It was not long before Gail was giving guitar lessons too. Chaos reigned when her extra English students arrived at the flat half an hour late, and the guitar pupils arrived half an hour early!

Hans, a Dutch engineer, who became a dear family friend, helped Gail with all the paper- work when her three month visa expired and she had to replace it with a work permit. He kept a fatherly eye on the whole team, giving them chocolate treats from time to time, because he did not consider they fed them-selves properly.

One Saturday it rained and Gail joined a group of friends on the beach. The waves were enormous – too big to body surf, but they had piggy back fights on the sand, and bopped on the sea wall to a ghetto blaster, behaving like real idiots because no-one was around – or so they thought. Gail was extremely embarrassed on Monday morning when one of her students said he had seen her on the beach on Saturday. This was a side of teaching she found difficult in a relatively small community – her students were everywhere.

The children's church at home collected money for Bibles which Gail gave to people in the Mozambican church she attended who had no money to buy their own, in the hospital, to her students and anyone who ·asked, like the Havanna trained teacher, and the Muslim teacher in her school who were searching for 'truth'.

By August the team was still looking for alternative accommodation, and many changes were taking place in Mozambique. There was talk of peace, and the Communist regime was falling apart following the death of President Samora Machel. On the occasion of Beira's 102nd Anniversary the authorities removed the ugly Marxist centrepiece and reconstructed the original fountain in the central square. It was a joy to see water in it, and the YWAM team joined the Baptist Church street witnessing and handing out tracts for the first time in many, many years.

Dellanie was due to return home to New Zealand, but before leaving, she and Gail had a short holiday in Zambia and Malawi. They had a great time together, often resorting to local 'chicken' buses for transport. One day waiting at a bus stop, they were offered a lift in a luxurious, air conditioned car. What a pleasure. Gail missed her soulmate, especially on trips to the beach.

Martin, from England, working with Global Literature Lifeline in Beira was one of the Saturday afternoon beach gang, and a friendship started developing between him and Gail. In October the team had to move from their flat, as the original tenants returned from leave, and with no other accommodation available, moved in with Nicky and Vic at the Manica Palace for five months.

After this they moved to a spacious flat in the centre of Beira. It caught the sea breeze, was above the worst noise of the streets below, and had three bathrooms! It was amazing that after the accommodation difficulties of the previous months all the girls were still on good terms, loving and supporting one another, teasing and being teased. Lots of fun and understanding had been part of it, but their YWAM training and experience had also laid strong foundations in each of them, allowing them to cope and retain a sense of humour. Once settled in their new accommodation, the flow of visitors, birthday celebrations, guitar and extra English lessons began again. Often at the end of the day, when Anneke was doing the final clearing up, Gail would ask her 'Can I do anything?', looking beyond her own needs and responsibilities to others also tired at the end of a busy day. Gail's light would still be on after everyone else was asleep, while she spent time with her Lord, planning the next day with Him. A Bible study was started for some of Gail's school students – something she had desired ever since she arrived in the school, and Anneke began making a video of the YWAM work in Beira aimed at helping people catch the vision and volunteer to join the team. Sadly, Marta had to go back to Brazil because her mother was ill.

Towards the end of the school year, Gail found the examination system really different. If students had a certain average for the year's work, they automatically passed to the next year, and they did not have to write exams. This meant everyone wanted extra marks to raise their averages, without working for them. She felt horribly caught in the middle, knowing that if they did not pass, they would be sent for military training the following year.

When the Mozambican nurses went on strike for a pay rise, the clinics closed and the Beira Central Hospital was kept running by expatriates and missionaries. Some of the sick children were orphans, and had no one to feed and look after them. Gail's team discovered if they didn't do this, no one would. This was a bit difficult for Gail. She wanted to get involved, but not being a medical worker, didn't know how she could help. Anneke solved her dilemma by asking Gail to keep the team supplied with coffee, which she did willingly, glad she could be useful in the midst of such a crisis.

In January 1990 a missionary in Beira mentioned to the team that there was a big, old, very run down building for sale in the centre of town. Anneke and Mike Oman, Regional Director of YWAM at that time, had a look at it. He saw it had potential, but Anneke felt depressed. Later, as the team waited to hear what God thought about it, Gail said 'I think the Lord says "Go for it".' The majority of the team agreed, and it was decided to buy the building.

She was back to 'chief cook and bottle washer' for two weeks when the Mozambican teachers were on strike and school was suspended. As a volunteer teacher, she was not involved in this action, but she would still walk the half hour to school to find out what was going on, and whether any directives had arrived from Maputo, the capital. It was a sociable time for Gail, visiting fellow teachers who were all 'bored out of their trees', as she put it, and wanting to get back to work. The final result was a great big zero – the government did not give anyone anything they asked for, and school resumed with the teachers conditions unaltered. A multitude of teachers at school wanted to learn English, and the only time they were free was Saturday afternoons. Gail started teaching them, although she did miss her time on the beach.

Life in Beira was never straightforward. The water pump broke, so the flat had no water, and when the lift ropes burnt out, water had to be carried up five flights of stairs. There were no lights or windows in the stairwell, and often children living on the lower floors would defecate on the stairs.

Several times Gail travelled home to attend friends' weddings and it always amazed the rest of the team how she was able to get free flights to and from Zimbabwe exactly when she needed them. She particularly enjoyed attending her friend Karen's wedding in Harare, when she became Mrs Ken Flower and Martin took the photograph appearing on the front cover of this book. Richmond, long acquainted with Gail, and working in Malawi, began visiting Beira quite frequently, and some rivalry began between him and Martin. Later Martin did a YWAM DTS in Norway, and Richmond did one in South Africa, and they both married beautiful Christian ladies other than Gail.

Gail developed a four-month theory – that after their first four months 'in the field' missionaries took a psychological dive, struggling with themselves and their jobs for a longer or shorter time, depending on their personalities. Fortunately Gail's home and family were near enough to help not only her but others overcome these times, and provide a place of rest and recreation.

During August a Swedish YWAM outreach team worked in Beira and took all Gail's school lessons one day – in English, of course. They sang, did drama, gave testimonies, and Gail was encouraged at how much her students understood. The pupils had opportunity to ask questions, some of them quite tough and deep, and at the end of the week the same team took a Bible study at which 18 students became Christians. Gail was ecstatic and prayed she would disciple them wisely and faithfully and get them firmly grounded in God's Word.

Gail and Debbie began making contact with some of the Beira street kids, taking them to the beach to swim and have fun. They were also giving three of them one meal a day, and letting them shower at the flat. Gail started sending urgent requests home for shirts, shorts and any other kind of boys clothing.

The street kids ran away from any form of discipline, preferring the harsh life on the streets of Beira, to the orphanage in Dondo. More children joined the original three and the team began praying for God's plan for them in 1991. Whenever the street kids were given new clothes, they would come back the next day with dirty, torn ones. Apparently older boys would bully them into giving up their clothes to sell, exchanging them for old ones. After this happened several times, Gail and Debbie told the boys if they kept giving their clothes away they would not get any more. For several weeks all was well, then suddenly it started all over again. Gail and Debbie then found that one of the boys, Vincente, had family in Beira and his father was the General of all the 'Bandidos'!

This family did not have a house, but slept on the streets, and the father held enough authority that he could order someone killed if they got in his way. Whenever the boys got new clothes, and Vincente's father sent people to take them, everyone was so afraid of him, they would not resist. Now the team was tangling with the 'Mafia' of Beira! They prayed for protection for the boys, and for themselves, and that Vincente's father would meet the living God and have his heart changed. At this point Gail notified the high school she would not be teaching there the following year. Her two year undertaking was at an end.

World Vision sent a container of medical supplies for YWAM to distribute in hospitals, clinics and pharmacies in their province. Anneke and Gail went to the tuberculosis and leprosy clinics to distribute toothbrushes and toothpaste. They had to give a demonstration of what to do with them, and it was highly entertaining watching some of the old wrinkled women trying to follow their instructions. They also took supplies to the orphanage and clinic in Dondo, the prison, and the school for the blind. As usual they took the opportunity to sing and share Jesus with everyone as well.

Gail came home for her sister Lindsay's 21st birthday. She left Beira very early in the morning and we were praying for her safety when she walked through the front door at 8 that night. Carol, our youngest daughter, had surprised us by walking through that same front door unexpectedly during the afternoon. She had been on a year long Rotary Exchange program in Colorado, USA, and decided to come home a month early, if she could arrive on her sister's birthday. What a reunion!

Before Anneke returned from leave in Holland in

January, 1991, she tried to telephone her travel details to us but could not get through. She had mentioned her plans to Gail, in passing, five weeks before, and was astounded to see Gail arrive to collect her at the airport. Gail simply said 'I thought I'd better come and see.' Later that month while trying to regain dominion over the cockroaches in the flat in Beira, God confirmed to Anneke, Debbie, and Gail His plan for YWAM to work with the Beira street children, in association with the local churches. This new project coincided with the end of a decade of Youth With A Mission work in South Central Africa – Zimbabwe, Mozambique, Zambia and Malawi.

Gail announced she would be going to Hawaii in the middle of the year, taking a six week course in teaching English to foreign students at the YWAM University of the Nations. She did not fully understand why she felt so strongly she should do this course, or where the finances would come from, but trusted that God would provide all she would need. Meanwhile Gail visited her old school in Beira to find they were two English teachers short, so offered her services three afternoons a week. Two of the boys ran away from the orphanage in Dondo, so classes were started for them in the YWAM flat during the mornings. Anneke, the pioneer, left to spy out the land in Quelimane, in northern Mozambique, and Gail and Debbie assumed responsibility for all the work in Beira.

Pastor Bonga, leading the indigenous church Gail attended, and who strongly supported the work YWAM was doing in Beira, invited Gail's father to speak in his church, and teach the local pastors. What a special time that was; father teaching and daughter translating the Word of God together.

The Beira team news letter of May 1991 said:

> 'You don't have to look hard to find ragged, dirty boys, sleeping on the pavements, digging in the piles of rubbish, hanging around the markets, shops, and restaurants, hoping for something to eat. Many have been separated from their families because of the war, or have social problems at home, and prefer living on the streets. We are planning to buy the old pharmacy building and turn it into a home, a primary school, a day/ family counselling centre for the street children of Beira. It is **very** exciting and we hope to start renovating in July.'

The man in charge of the orphanage in Dondo did a lot of damage to it while drunk one day, and this place was closed, making the need for a centre in Beira more urgent than ever.

Whenever Gail came home, we tried to let her rest and sleep in as much as possible, but it was never long before she was telephoning friends and making arrangements to see them and do things. It was a regular social whirl, when she wasn't racing around shopping for all the things people asked her to buy that were not available in Beira. Many times she would use her own money for these items, and often the recipients forgot to repay her. She would just smile and be glad she could do it for them.

Back in Beira Gail wrote:

> 'The parents' day went quite well, but on Monday we arrived at school and were told to announce that all the kids whose parents didn't pitch up, were suspended for the next two days. That's

quite heavy, 'coz if they miss a certain number of lessons they get chucked out of school, so there were lots of interesting situations to sort out. Then a couple of kids were given what is like a black mark – but it means that they won't ever be able to get a good behaviour mark on their report – which could affect their whole future. The problem was that the kids concerned aren't generally badly behaved and the whole class said that they didn't deserve it – so I had to try and sort that out – try reasoning logically and calmly in Portuguese, when you're between two different parties ranting and raving! I guess I'm finding it hard to find the line between being firm and disciplined and also just and fair and understanding – especially when kids are cheating etc. Anyway, it means I rely on God more and more. I'm convinced that He sent me here to sort out my life – not for the benefit of the people here at all! But I'm glad He cares that much about me.'

There were a few complications with Gail's passport. It was full, although it was not due for renewal. Fortunately the Foreign Affairs department in Harare was extremely helpful, and a new passport and all the required visas were ready for Gail to leave for Hawaii on 29th June 1991. In the early hours of that morning my 83-year-old father died, ending 70 fruitful years walking with God. Gail's life was mapped out for the next three exciting months, and we shared her excitement as we saw her off at the airport.

Hallelujah, hallelujah, hallelujah
Like a wave splashing onto the beach
Then running up the sand,
      smoothing,
            covering up the stones,
                  melting the sandcastle
                          walls
Your love runs over me, flows through me
Covers me.
Covers me - so that no one can see the
      stones that cause me to stumble,
  and the bumps and gaps are smoothed
over
And the walls that I've built up inside
      myself are washed away.

Let your living water sweep over my soul.
Let your Holy Spirit take control
Refresh me, revitalise me,
   renew my first love.
Awaken my Spirit
      and listen to the voice of the Lord.
and act on it
Be a servant, be humble
      be a child of the king!!!

What is it?

that makes me feel this way?
 Like a bear woken during hibernation
 Like a lioness defending her cubs
 Like a hyena giggling, mocking
 Like an orphan, alone, vulnerable
  longing for love
  asserting independence
  self sufficiency
  crying for a touch.
 Love   in a hardened heart
  trying to break out
   but not trying too hard
    lest it succeeds
 and the world sees the rain,
  the greyness, the dullness
   the death?
Why death?
 Where is the life?
Sunshine, laughter, smiles, a touch, a look
 — locked behind the iron bars
  encased in steel.
   Don't let me be vulnerable!

Gail aged three

Skiing in Italy

Carol   Rikki   Gail   Margaret   Lindsay
1985

100

Gail's boys

English class – Samora Machel School

*Carrying water
in Malawi*

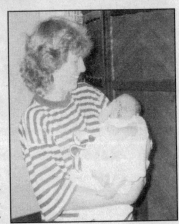

*Meeting
nephew
Bradley*

Engagement photosession

14th May 1994

Chapter 9

Trusting, Training and Travel

'Aloha! That's Hawaiian for Hello, and I'm here along with 70,000 other people who have come to see the total solar eclipse, 11th July, 1991 at 7.28 am. I hope it's clear to see.'

The eclipse was an extra gift for Gail amongst all the other wonderful experiences in such beautiful surroundings. The accommodation was luxurious in the extreme at the YWAM University of the Nations. She loved the Teaching English to Foreign Students Course, and even enjoyed the heavy load of home-work. It was a privilege to be with others who wanted to be more effective in reaching the world for Jesus. Youth With A Mission had a big outreach to the visitors in Hawaii during the week of the eclipse; in between, and as often as possible Gail was on the beach.

As with all YWAM schools, classroom and practical work went hand in hand and Gail not only taught English to Japanese students, but snorkelled with them, and toured beautiful Kona island and the

volcano with them as well. In one classroom discussion, Gail found her methods of teaching were very acceptable to the professional teachers, and was able to share some practical tips that helped all her fellow students. The six-week school in Hawaii went very quickly, and Gail would love to have stayed for more courses. Her ultimate goal was to acquire a degree through the YWAM University, and each course she undertook gave her points towards this. She was pleased to gain an 'A' when the school ended, but sad to have to say goodbye to new friends.

This was counter-balanced by the anticipation of travelling to Montrose, Colorado, to visit Laura from the original Beira team, now married to Paul Lloyd.

They lived in a trailer home, and Laura was expecting their first baby. After a short visit, Gail took the bus back to Denver through spectacular scenery. She passed Vail, where the 1988 world ski championships had been held, and on seeing the ski runs she longed for the feel of ski boots once more. Laura's family was wonderful, meeting Gail from the bus, and getting her to the airport at 5 in the morning for her next destination, Belo Horizonte in Brazil.

Gail was glad she did not have to stay overnight in New York as she found it very expensive, and the traffic overwhelming. Her plane was delayed in Sao Paulo for two hours, and as soon as she arrived in Rio de Janeiro a man lied to her about the banks being closed and she got ripped off when he changed some money for her. Thus her first impressions of Brazil were not good. However, Marta from the Beira team, had asked some of her friends to meet Gail in Belo Horizonte, and her pastor's wife delivered her safely to the YWAM 'Restoration House', where, much to her relief, she was expected.

Gail shared a small room on the main noisy corridor. She was a little scared of one of the 14 street boys living in the house as he wandered around the building shouting and wailing, until she discovered that he was deaf.

Gail worked in the 'Rescue House' where boys came to bath, eat and wash clothes. Her day started at 6.45 am and after breakfast of bread and sweet black coffee or tea, there would be an hour of intercession, half an hour of worship, and then assignments were given for the morning. The Rescue House did all the lunch and supper cooking for two other houses as well, which meant a great deal of vegetable preparation and dish washing. Lunch was always beans and rice, and supper was soup or macaroni. Before lunch the boys had a Bible study, and after lunch would help with cleaning before going to a nearby sports area. The staff went with them until 3 pm and returned to clean bathrooms or other areas until 4 pm.

A day or two after Gail arrived, the police rounded up all the street kids and put them in jail. They had been going about cutting women's hair and selling it for wigs! The children were older than those Gail was used to in Mozambique. They were into drugs, sniffing glue and thinners, and prostitution. A little boy of 9 or 10 came to the centre one day. He had been smoking and sniffing thinners at the same time. The thinners had burst into flame and the plastic container he was holding melted all over his fingers, giving him a horrible burn. They dressed his hand and took him back to his street corner, and as they watched he was immediately back to smoking again.

Gail visited the family of some of the kids, and was amazed at the living conditions – in one tiny room Mum, Dad and five children slept in three beds. The oldest child was 16, the youngest 4 months, and the mother was pregnant again. Gail met one of the street people whose 12-year-old daughter was pregnant. She saw everything on the streets of Belo Horizonte, and said nothing could shock her ever again.

Belo Horizonte was a big city, and Gail's guardian angel worked overtime as she hopped on and off buses, amongst the traffic. Marta saw Gail as much as her busy schedule permitted, taking her to her church, and away for a weekend. One night all the girls on the team had fun skating together. Over the first weekend of September, Gail became part of an international incident. On the Friday night a team went onto the streets to spend time with the kids as usual. They were playing dominos, singing and chatting, when a man stopped to talk to some of the team. He said they were doing a good work, and walked on. A short while later a police car zoomed past and around the corner, lights flashing and siren wailing. Next minute around the same corner walked a uniformed policeman with his gun in the air and a street kid by the scruff of the neck. He then started assaulting the kid. The man who had spoken to the group earlier turned out to be a policeman too. He reappeared and approached the girl he had been talking to, slapping her in the face. Gail turned to see if she was alright, and, in turn, he whacked Gail across the back of the neck, and then got hold of a Swedish girl and bent her hand behind her back. The team were all in shock when the original man said if he had a gun he would shoot them all! Then the policemen grabbed Mati, a Samoan on the team, and started hitting and kicking him, chasing the rest of the team off. The leader of the team jumped in a taxi to go and find a lawyer. The rest stayed and watched helplessly from a distance. Two more police cars arrived, and eventually the police loaded Mati into one and took him off, destination unknown.

The shocked team returned to the base, woke everyone up, and started to pray. After several hours Mati was located at one of the police stations. He was released at 5 am next morning and taken to hospital suffering from bruises and broken ribs. It transpired that one of the kids had stolen the plain clothes policeman's money, he decided that Mati was responsible, and that the team had encouraged the crime.

Although Saturday was supposed to be a day off, someone had to prepare lunch and supper, so Gail and a Brazilian girl were on duty – a lot of work for two people, especially as Gail was sneezing, coughing and heading for a dose of 'flu. Later that day, Marta dragged her miles across the city to spend the night with her – Gail thought she was going to die – but it was good because Marta fed her up and she slept all of Sunday which would have been impossible at the base. Marta preached about missions in a church on Sunday evening, and Gail's temperature disappeared. She spent another night with Marta, and returned to the base at lunchtime on Monday to find it in total chaos. The newspapers and television people had been there since Saturday, and Mati hardly had time to eat because of all the interviews. All the embassies of the different countries represented – eight nationalities in the team of eleven people – had been contacted, except for Zimbabwe, which did not have a representative in Brazil at that time.

To make things worse, two of the boys in the restoration house got into a fight. One pulled a knife on the other, and they both left the house, which made everyone very sad. One of them did return later in the day, to apologise and be restored, which was great, but it showed Gail, first hand, the constant battle that rages where street children are concerned. They can have Christian contact for years, and be doing really well, as was the case with these two boys, and suddenly Satan sneaks in and spoils it.

After a month in Brazil, Gail flew to Johannesburg for a brief visit with her Grandmother, before arriving home on the afternoon of 27th September.

A heart to know you?
  A heart to love,
          to desire,
          to thirst for
    your nearness
      to delight in hearing
          your voice, your word
              your plans, purposes
                joys, sorrows.
  To count the cost,
      to lose my life
          to empty myself
    and consider it all joy,
        a priviledge
        an honour.
  Is it there... this heart?
      dedicated, disciplined, desirous
        of you?
  It's hard to find,
      it loses itself in people
        work, leisure, religion

It wanders through the forests
of the world and its
clutter
Waiting for a clearing
Waiting for new strength
waiting
waiting
Waiting for you to sieze me,
o God,
to light the fire
to renew the love
to restore the joy
the strength
the desire.

Create in me ... o God ----
a pure heart,
Renew a steadfast spirit within me
Do not cast your Holy Spirit from me,
Restore to me the joy of your salvation
and grant me a willing spirit
to sustain me.

Chapter 10

Casa Ré-om – The House of the Lord, My Shepherd

'It's not just a puncture, the wheel came off.'

The old YWAM vehicle had been in Zimbabwe for extensive repairs, and over the August public holiday weekend Lindsay and her friend Stephen, Gail and I, drove to Mutare together to collect it and drive through to Beira the next day. Not far into Mozambique the truck hit a huge pothole with an enormous jolt, which caused the engine to die. Lindsay and Stephen following behind managed to avoid the hole, and together we eventually got the truck started again. From then on, however, the engine refused to run smoothly.

While driving through the next town, Chimoio, a 4×4 Land Cruiser travelling in the opposite direction suddenly turned across the road in front of us without warning. Gail's defensive driving, quick reflexes, and God's grace got us through the only available space left to go, and miraculously there were no pedestrians in the way. Stephen and Lindsay said they could hardly believe their eyes.

Just through the next town, Gondola, the truck suddenly wobbled, and we heard an ominous sound. Gail stopped on the verge, expecting to find nothing worse than a puncture. The entire back wheel had disappeared and was found twenty minutes later in the middle of a nearby maize field. This time Stephen and Lindsay could hardly stand they were laughing so much. The wheel was returned to us by a group of local children who thought the whole episode highly amusing. The axle hub was too hot to handle, and the wheel rim somewhat bent. The only thing to do was load all the luggage from the truck into Stephen's car, and drive the short distance to Maforga Mission Farm for help. Roy Perkins returned to the truck with Stephen and they repaired it sufficiently to drive it to the farm for further repair, borrowing one nut from each of the three remaining wheels to secure the fourth in place.

We set off again, the truck still stalling every time we slowed down – a frequent occurrence owing to the extremely poor condition of the road. After an hour of this frustrating driving, Gail said we ought to turn back. We were roughly half-way between the farm and Beira, and after a quick conference, we decided it made more sense to press on and have the vehicle looked at in Beira, rather than stagger the greater distance back to the border. We prayed that the engine would behave itself, and from that point on had no further problems with it, finally arriving in Beira nine weary hours after leaving Zimbabwe – a journey which normally took three hours.

The Muslim mechanic in Beira, to whom Gail took the truck asked her where she had come from. 'Zimbabwe,' she said. 'That's impossible,' he said. 'A vehicle in this condition could never have been driven so far. How did you manage to get here?' What an opportunity for Gail to witness to the goodness of her God.

While Gail had been at home waiting for the vehicle repairs, she had worked hard on an impressive document setting out the complete project she and Debbie planned to develop in Beira. Before coming home Debbie and Gail had spent two days shut away in the flat fasting, praying and planning. This included the purpose, objectives and goals for using the building that had so depressed Anneke, as a Day Centre for the street kids, a home for 20 of them, a school, staff accommodation, and offices from which to counsel and initiate parent contact, and to re-habilitate children back into their own families where possible. They planned a projected timetable, all the equipment required, alterations to the build-ing, estimated costs, and manpower needed. Church evangelism and training was also proposed, and they planned to open a coffee bar as well. This was presented to YWAM leaders, to the Social Action Department of the Province, and to Greystone Park Fellowship church leaders. A staggering undertaking for two twenty-six year olds.

Gail wrote a letter from Beira, dated 17th October 1991:

> 'It's great being back – I'm enjoying myself living in total chaos ... It's nice to see the boys again – although there are some new ones, and others have disappeared ... Yesterday Debs and I and one of the pastor's daughters armed ourselves with broom, dustpan and brush, old clothes and working gloves, and moved all the medicines in the basement of the Pharmacy to a huge heap by

the stairs ... it took us the day – was very disgusting – we found a dead kitten and a couple of fossilized rats. Anyway, it's done now, so when the medicines are moved out we'll start trying to dismantle the shelves and scrub and paint the walls – any helpers very welcome!'

Meanwhile, back in the flat:

'We had the biggest flood yet – the kids had turned the shower tap on, and the water must have come on at about 5.00 am so by the time Debs staggered through to the kitchen, the lounge and dining room were partially submerged. The carpet smells awful, but is drying slowly.'

Negotiations for YWAM to purchase the Pharmacy building dragged on, and the building structure was checked by experts to ascertain how much repair work would be necessary. Most of the roof timbers appeared to be sound, but the roof had been leaking badly in some places, and the first floor balcony columns needed major reconstruction.

The first floor interior was in an unbelievable condition filled with all manner of rubbish, except for two rooms occupied by illegal squatters, and with gaping holes in the floorboards and ceilings. The bathroom was unusable, the bath the only unbroken item, and the kitchen was a dismal black hole without basic fixtures. Debbie and Gail thought it was wonderful.

It was not long before a work team from Greystone Park Fellowship was dismantling the medicine racks in the basement, and painting the walls a happy yellow – the first of many working trips from Gail's home church in Harare.

Once the purchase price had been paid in full, thanks largely to tremendous fund raising efforts overseas, the renovation work continued. Sadly, the pharmacist refused to move out, even after all the relevant documents had been legally signed. He remained, illegally, hampering the expansion of the work by occupying his chemist shop on the ground floor.

After Debbie and Gail had both fallen through different parts of the first floor, its repair became top priority. Various individuals and Discipleship Training School outreach teams made steady progress on restoring the building, and the vision became a reality.

By this time the girls had contact with about fifty street kids. The boys would come to the flat in groups of ten to bath, wash their clothes, cook food, play games, receive medical attention, do some school work, listen to Bible Stories and pray together.

Christmas Eve 1991 Gail, Debbie and the boys spent their first night in the Pharmacy building. And what a night it turned out to be. It was more than a little primitive, and the food went 'off' because of the heat and humidity. Mozambique does not celebrate Christmas but the 25th December is 'Family Day'. It was significant that YWAM Beira should celebrate the birth of their new 'family' as the Christian world celebrated the birth of Jesus. But just as with any family there was a lot of work to be done. Next morning Debbie cleaned up the chaos in the flat, left from the boys' evening bath session, while Gail cleaned up various piles of diarrhoea from corners of the house because the kids got sick from the food.

The long-awaited move from the flat to the pharmacy building was made at the end of January with the boys carrying boxes porter style from one to the other. Unfortunately the first floor of the building was not secure, and much of the property was stolen during the three days of moving, before Gail and Debbie were on the spot to keep an eye on things. Both Gail and Debbie felt God was testing them – were they prepared to keep going, whatever the cost? They considered, and said '**Yes**' and from then on God poured out blessing upon blessing. We had long prayed that God would raise up men to share the Beira burden with Gail and Debbie, and soon Joe came from America, Thomas from Germany, and Mike from England.

Waiting for permission to do major renovations to the building, was frustrating. Each new project had to be officially approved, slowing progress considerably at times. Many of the supplies were bought in Zimbabwe and transported to Beira, often causing further delays. Thomas was wonderful in finding necessary items locally, and bargaining for them in his limited Portuguese, or just making things from scratch.

By February the school started. The Department of Education approved the classroom facilities and registered the school purely on the strength of Gail's certificate from her six week course in Hawaii! 20 children started in the Grade 1 class, and 10 in Grade 2, taught by Mozambican teachers, with Gail overseeing the teaching and meting out discipline. She became very handy with a wooden spoon, and the children loved and respected her.

A small Anglican Church in Harare began a Job Creation Scheme, training well-educated but unemployed young Zimbabwean Christians to teach English as a foreign language, placing them in schools in Mozambique. Gail and Debbie accepted the extra work and the challenge of helping with this project from the start, and not only housed the teachers placed in Beira, but warned them of the problems, and encouraged them continuously. As a direct result of this, God challenged Nyasha Gombo, one of the teachers on this project, to do a YWAM Discipleship Training School in Zambia. She is now back at Casa Ré-om as a member of staff, and doing a great job.

January and February are always the hottest months of the year in Beira, and the mosquitoes are at their worst. The humidity also rises very high. Gail began suffering from severe athlete's foot which was difficult to control in the heat and unhygienic conditions. She would come home with nasty mouth ulcers too, probably due to the somewhat basic diet, and stress, but she never complained. In five years she took no malaria prophylactics, and she never suffered from it.

The school rapidly expanded, and there was a never ending need for clothes for the students. God always supplied sufficient food, money, medicines or transport when it was needed. The children learnt to pray for these things, and would get really excited seeing their prayers answered. Very few girls enrol in Escola Ré-om because they are employed as domestic help or baby minders.

Gail and Debbie were soon looking for another house in which to start an orphanage. One was found in Manga, on the inland side of Beira. At the time it was occupied by Government Forces – Frelimo – and had many bullet holes in the walls marking the frequent attacks from the opposing forces – Renamo. It was an ideal building, and the owner was keen that it be used for an orphanage, but the continued Renamo attacks were cause for concern, and because of this, and the lack of suitable personnel to establish it, the project was deferred.

Debbie did a YWAM Leadership School in Kenya and was away for three months, and during this time, Gail facilitated a television quality video of the YWAM work in Beira, called *Beira's Buried Treasures*. Gail said on the video 'The most important part of the whole Beira project is that people pray regularly for individual kids.' They could see the changes in the children who were being prayed for. They would attend school more regularly, try harder, ask questions, and some of their behaviour problems improved. When complete the film was distributed to YWAM bases worldwide, in the hope that it would encourage people to join the team. South African television showed extracts on prime viewing time, resulting in a great deal of interest from people all over the Republic, and some donations to the work.

Red Cross and UNICEF took an interest in the project, and offered some food support which was very welcome. Ginny, working in Beira with Global Literature Lifeline, started sewing classes with some of the boys, and Wendy, Christine and Lynda, came from a YWAM Discipleship Training School in England for a three month outreach. Through it all, Gail as their team leader, smiled. For a while Wendy thought she was laughing at 'the pommies' as Gail called them, but then she realised her smile was a permanent fixture. She was a great team leader, but struggled to balance leading the team with running the whole Beira project as well.

Wendy developed such a love for the people of Mozambique, that at the end of her outreach she talked to Gail about coming back. She thought she had given Gail quite a hard time, and was shocked that Gail got excited at the possibility of her returning. To Wendy's question 'What on earth can I do in Mozambique?' Gail gave a long list of many things. Six months later Wendy was back, for two years. They never had disagreements, but Wendy considered their relationship rather one-sided. Gail was always there to lean on in times of trouble, and to talk to whenever needed, but Gail would struggle through any difficulties of her own alone. Eventually Wendy confronted Gail about this, and brought about something of a turning-point in their relationship, but vulnerability was never Gail's strong point.

It was a day of celebration when electricity was installed in the pharmacy building, although the supply was often irregular. Water was a constant problem. The major supply of fresh water to Beira is the Pungwe River flowing from the Eastern Highlands of Zimbabwe. During recent years of drought in the region, the river ran very low and the pumping station could not operate for up to eight weeks at a time. Fortunately the wells in Beira are common property, and with the use of a cart fitted with several large water containers the boys would eagerly volunteer to fetch water. When the water did eventually come through the pipes it was often brackish or salty as the sea backwashed up the river estuary. Gail and others delighted in coming 'home' to running water, showers and baths. Water problems were partly eased when two large asbestos storage tanks were installed in the basement of the building. These automatically filled when the water was switched on, although obvious limits on the use of this water still had to be strictly observed.

Crises were always happening. One day the guard on the block of flats where the girls used to live, tried to kill Tome by throwing him in the river. He arrived at the Pharmacy soaking wet, but still alive. Another time, one of the boys was attacked by a machete-wielding adult, and as he threw his arm up in self-protection, his thumb was all but severed from his hand. Several have been hurt falling off the back bumpers of motor cars while illegally hitching rides. Soon a number of boys started sleeping on the stairs and the upstairs verandah of the pharmacy building, away from the danger of the streets. The pressure of responsibility was constant, from as early as 5 in the morning until sometimes after 11 at night. Once a telephone was installed the ability to communicate with people in Beira and elsewhere made a big difference to everyone on the base. Often there was no time, peace and quiet, or energy for letter writing, and phone calls took their place.

For the staff, there was a never ending daily variety: waiting for official meetings to begin, negotiating permission for this or that, sorting out fights, doctoring hurts, trips to the hospital, loving the sensitive ones, disciplining the wayward, contacting families, dealing with emergencies, entertaining visitors, or housing work teams. Once 35 Teen Missions teenagers and their leaders spent five weeks at Casa Ré-om changing partitions, fixing ceilings and painting themselves and some of the walls.

The noise from the street, or neighbouring families, never ceased. One night in particular, Gail was exhausted, but sleep was impossible because of a rowdy party next door. Eventually, in utter frustration she grabbed a wooden spoon, went onto the verandah and ran it along some corrugated iron, to get the attention of the party goers, and ask them to quieten down. In their drunken state, two of the men accused Gail of 'shooting' at them, and threatened to shoot her legs which they could see through the balustrade. She knew this was no idle threat as many were still armed from the years of war, and not afraid to use their weapons. She really thought her final hour had come! Fortunately they soon forgot about her, and continued with their celebrations, and Gail crept back to bed, thankful that she was still in one piece.

The gift of a computer arrived from England, and

this helped with much of the day-to-day running of the base. Gail dreamed of getting a number of computers – obsolete so quickly in western countries and often thrown on the scrap heap – in order to create opportunities for the children in the school to become computer literate. Their chances of achieving something significant would be increased many fold if they had a knowledge of English and computer skills. This is one dream yet to be fulfilled.

In July 1992 Gail's younger sister, Carol, dropped the bombshell on the family that she was 10 weeks pregnant. I agonized for two weeks over how to break the news to Gail. Debbie was away, and Gail was still carrying all the responsibility of the Beira base. I eventually had to write, because a work team was going down from our church, and Gail needed to know before someone said something to her. She was shattered. It took her several days to get over the shock, but she was very supportive of Carol, writing her a card full of love and encouragement. She adored her nephew Bradley, making a special trip home to see him soon after he was born on 10th February 1993, and showed off his photographs at every opportunity.

The Red Cross made a building available where many of the street kids were able to sleep in safety, and leave their few possessions during the day. Gail was always distressed by the kids living conditions when they slept rough, sometimes making cardboard shelters for themselves, but never having any permanency. The work with street children is ever changing. It is a constant 'one step forward, two steps back' situation. Some will attend school regularly and do really well, and then suddenly go back to the streets, or hitch-hike to another town up country, just for fun. For others, the call of the street life is too strong, or they are bullied into stealing by the older boys, and then are too ashamed to return. Others get hooked on drugs, or into a gang. Yet others come to know Jesus as Saviour in a very real way and really try to break with their past.

Fun and creative times will always get a response, and a successful day centre was started, providing things for the children to do during the school holidays, or for those who were not enrolled in school. They spent time gluing, painting, cutting up, and creating the kind of things young boys the world over enjoy. Playing football, trips to the beach, or just singing and talking, reading and playing games are popular, too. Sometimes they just want to climb up beside an adult and hold a hand, or just sit close, feeling secure, knowing that someone really cares. Then there are those special days with treats of sweets, biscuits or orange juice.

Debbie and Gail used to have prayer walks round the central square on Sunday nights where the local Hindu population congregated. One Friday afternoon they met with other missionaries to pray for Beira in the square and the kids joined them. Gail was moved to tears as she shared in her home church how the boys spontaneously began to pray for the city of Beira not caring who saw or heard. What joy, what encouragement – it was **all** worth it – the seed that had been planted was beginning to bear fruit.

A British Army training contingent stationed in the eastern border region of Zimbabwe decided to split the proceeds of a fun run from Mutare to Beira between an orphanage in Zimbabwe, and Casa Ré-om, in Beira. They raised a staggering amount of money and were able to purchase mattresses, blankets, medicines, a fridge and freezer, and other essential items for the centre. There was an official presentation, speeches and balloons in the central square in Beira, amidst quite a carnival atmosphere. A very practical exercise, thoroughly enjoyed by all.

As peace slowly returned to Mozambique, following years of bitter armed struggle, foreign aid began to pour in, compounds for foreign workers were built, and many more shops opened, making shopping much easier. Prices are high – at least twice as expensive as in Zimbabwe – but it was nice to get things locally, and not have everything sent from Harare. Even ice cream became available, and several restaurants opened their doors. The YWAM staff enjoy an occasional meal out together, especially if there is a birthday to celebrate. Taking the kids for an ice cream became a popular treat, or special reward.

Much had changed – hostilities were at an official end; YWAM had an established, on-going project in the poorest country in the world; some of the children had been reunited with their families that war had divided; the street children now had the opportunity of education, and a future as responsible citizens and leaders of a new, free nation. But Gail also saw the urgent need for qualified people to reach those still suffering mentally, emotionally and spiritually, from the horrors of war, family rejection, and poverty, and she wanted to do something about it. She decided to study some more.

Oh Lord how I love you
When I look at the blueness of the sky
And the white fluffiness of the clouds
    I think of your faithfulness
    I am assured
        of your amazing love
How unworthy I am to have a God —
            like you

Who never
        turns away from me
Always listens
Always cares

How can I be so stubborn,
        independent
    lethargic?
How can I "do my own thing"
    ignoring you
        struggling in the mud
Getting tired,
      so tired .....

Those who wait on you
        will renew their strength
They will mount up with wings
      as Eagles
They will run
      and not be weary
They will walk
      and not faint
O Lord — Create a clean heart within me
      Renew a right spirit
Restore to me
      the joy of your salvation
And lead me in your ways
    forever
        more !!

Chapter 11

Canada

'I'm going to Canada in September.'

God had spoken to Gail about the three month YWAM CIN – Children In Need School in Winfield, British Columbia, and remembering how He got her to Hawaii and Brazil, we agreed this would be so.

During the morning of the day she was due to leave, we asked her how much money she still needed. 'Oh, about Z$5000, but I know God told me to go, so I'm going even without enough to pay the school fees.' At eleven o'clock that morning she was given a cheque for Five Hundred British Pounds, which, when converted, gave her exactly Z$5000! Her face was a study of joy and relief and she admitted 'Phew, I wish God wouldn't do this to me.' We agreed.

Gail broke her journey in Toronto, where Joan, our YWAM friend of many years, met her and drove her to see Niagara Falls. She enjoyed a few days lazing around and going 'window shopping'. The maple trees were beginning to show their autumn colours as the weather turned cooler, but she missed seeing them in all their famous glory as she travelled further west.

She was grateful to Peter, who spent his DTS outreach in Beira helping fix the pharmacy building roof, for meeting her in Vancouver, and driving her to Winfield before the school started. Gail's welcome card in Winfield, read:

'You did not choose me, but I chose you and appointed you to go and bear fruit – fruit that will last. Then the Father will give you whatever you ask in my name.'
(John 15:16)

and her first diary entry reads:

'18th September 1993

Dear God
I'm sitting here on a rocky beach on the shores of the Okanagan Lake ... it's an amazing thing – 150 miles long, the water is clean and icy cool ... it's very quiet and peaceful, just the lapping of the water ... the occasional aeroplane passing ... I'm with Lynda ... I've been talking a lot about You ... Your goodness and faithfulness and the amazing things You do ... I just love knowing You ... I love walking with You ... it's so much fun ... so fulfilling and challenging too!

I just wanted to thank You for bringing me here to CIN, to Canada, this beautiful place. Thank You for all those people who gave sacrificially so I could be here ... please bless and repay each of them **abundantly**! It's a humbling thing for me, to receive such blessing – I know I don't deserve it ... but I do receive it and thank You! You know, it's kind of fun to write to You ... I hope You enjoy it too!

Another thing I want to thank You for is my family ... You know what's in my heart for them ... and Debs and Wend etc., I won't write it all here ... but I thank You. I thank You too, for taking me out of my small glass bowl and putting me in this big tank with all these other fishes ... help me to be humble, and learn from them and all You've done in their lives.

What I'd really like to see happening in my life during this time, is that I would learn to affirm and encourage others, to build them up in all wisdom and understanding ... I'd like to become more open ... to chat and get to know other people more freely ... to be able to laugh and joke, but not in a way that exalts myself and puts them down. I guess I'm just asking to be more relaxed and confident in myself so that I can edify and share with others.

I also need to be equipped for dealing better with the skids and their problems ... as well as in leading the team! I guess in short, I'm asking that you give me wisdom and understanding to counsel others, and create a more open, and giving and loving heart in me.

And, whatever else You want to do in me, or through me, Father ... I give You full permission to go ahead ... I want **all** You have for me here in this place ... that I wouldn't let any opportunities go wasted ... that I would gain the maximum according to Your perfect will.

Thank You for loving me, for choosing me ... help me to bear fruit for You that will last...

With all my love and heart
Your daughter, Gaily'

School began on 23rd September. Gail enjoyed presenting her collage of the significant things in her life to her class. The stories from the rest of the class often stunned her, she cried in some, and saw God's amazing grace and love in others. She felt humbled and awed at the stable family background God had given her.

Her work duty was translating for Christina from Brazil. She wrote 'it drains my brain and really frustrates me.' She had to pray for grace, patience and creative ways to help Christina understand the teaching. Her other room mates were Anna from Sweden and Ellen from Norway. Gail appreciated the cosy feeling Ellen's Scandinavian influence gave to their room, with her table cloth and 'tea candles'. Three of them had pictures of their respective street kids stuck up on the walls, giving them the same 'heart beat' and reason for being in Winfield. Gail soon became resident English teacher in the room, and enjoyed the openness as they shared what God was doing in their lives.

Gail, and several other students began walking a 5km circuit each day, which was lots of fun, good exercise in beautiful surroundings, and a time to share together and get to know one another better. Gail and Jani also managed to initiate a water war which constantly found them dripping wet and mopping up, amid much hilarity.

Teaching began with a child's world – by understanding your childhood, family and relationships. The lecturer asked each student to write a letter to their dads. Gail enjoyed doing it because it was such a positive thing for her; it wasn't for a lot of people. When she returned home, she gave it to him – this is what she wrote:

131

'21st September, 1993

Dear Dad,

I'm doing this CIN course, and we've been told it would do us good to write to our Dads ... all the things we've never told you!

I've been listening to others sharing about their Dads ... all I can say, is that you've probably been the greatest blessing that God has put into my life – and that's the truth!

I wonder if you could ever understand the amazement I feel, when I think of what you went through when mom was killed ... and that you kept me ... more than that, you cared for me and brought me up, and gave me a new mother and family ... I want to thank you for that ... I want to tell you that I deeply admire and respect you, as a man, for looking after me ... I know it must have been extremely difficult, often!

As I was growing up ... I remember "romping" with you on the carpet by the fire; playing chess; you letting me beat you without me knowing; you explaining patiently my physics and chemistry homework; you, giving me Latin assignments in Germany, and art, too.

I remember you wanting to take me skiing ... to experience and enjoy so many different things.

How can I ever thank you for "bribing" me to play the guitar at G.P. – that has been so much fun for me ... I would have missed out on so much, if you hadn't done that. I wish, when we were in Germany, that you'd sent me to a German School. I know I would have loathed it ... but I always regret not being forced into learning German – I feel it was a lost opportunity ... but then you weren't to know how much I enjoy languages now!

My growing up has been full of happy memories, and for these I thank you, and I thank God, too!

I remember the only time I remember you getting mad at me – that time when we went to a rally or something and didn't let you know when it ended late ... so you had to come and fetch us, and then take all my friends home – I cried, but not because you were angry, but because I'd angered you! I remember when you used to gate me for coming home late ... and then let me go out anyway. Mom thought you were too soft on me ... I just know that you loved me!

Do you remember when I left to go to England with Sogs (Karen) ... I was so sad and scared to be leaving. And when I met you in England when I'd just come back from Sweden, and I was so confused and lonely ... and you let me cry, and held me.

Sometimes I get the feeling that you think I've grown up now, and I don't need you to be my Dad so much. Like a few months ago at church when we had communion and you said for fathers to serve their families ... and I so much wanted to take communion with you ... but you were being the 'pastor'. I didn't take communion that day ... I cried! I understand though, too ... I'm like you in so many ways ... I hide in my work, I find fulfilment in that ... rather than exposing myself and admitting that I'm lonely and afraid.

Dad, sometimes ... more often recently ... I'm really scared for you ... I mean, really scared ... you work and work ... you counsel, you pastor, you care ... you're always there for others, then you take time out and drive to fetch me from the border ... even though your back is causing you so much pain ... I love it when you do that – because it shows me that you're my Dad, and not my 'pastor'. But ... it's not right, the way I see it ... that you carry so much by yourself. I see you being 'burnt out'. I wish you'd say **'No'** and take time for yourself ... you need to love yourself in order to love others. I don't mean to lecture you ... I love you, and you scare me ... I know I'm almost 28 years old, and I run a project for street kids and have a lot of responsibility ... but I still need a Dad ... inside I'm still a little girl ... who wants to be loved and held by her Daddy. I don't care what you are and what you do ... I just want you to be my Dad ... and I don't want you to kill yourself doing it!

I want to end by saying again ... you're the greatest blessing God has given me ... and I love you, I honour you, I respect and admire you, for the amazing, selfless, man of God you are! Thank you for being my Dad ... please, please, look after yourself. I love you.

Your daughter, and I hope, friend, Gail.'

It was over three weeks before Gail received any letters from home. When they finally arrived she was so excited she jumped up and down like a three-year-old. She was already feeling overwhelmed by the material they were studying and its personal impact on her life. She wasn't digesting it, she got behind with her first book report, and really missed home and Mozambique.

The very next day was 'Affirmation' day. The class played a game like musical chairs – the one left without a chair stood in the middle and was affirmed by the others. Gail was said to be an encourager, strong and stable, committed, they liked her smile, her 'wildness' and her ability to have fun and be serious. Someone said she looked like a 'whole' person – she really enjoyed that and said she felt 'whole'. God knew just what Gail needed to hear just then. During one walk Gail and Jani got into a deep spiritual discussion about heaven, but they soon balanced these heavenly thoughts with a pine needle and water fight.

Not far into the course, Gail's room mates had to pray together for better sleep; nightmares were frequent as people worked through deep problems they had experienced in their lives. Gail was missing the 'skids' as she sometimes referred to the street kids in Mozambique and felt God's concern for them. She cried over them.

Early in October the CIN had to pack up and move to a barn, as their accommodation was required for a weekend camp. The barn was immaculately furnished, and made everyone feel like one big happy family. They could watch television, play the piano, write, read, chat and laugh together. Gail's 28th birthday was celebrated there, too, with crazy presents, lots of balloons, a birthday book signed by everyone in the church at home, a bowl of flowers from Thomas in Germany, and Polly threw her in the muddy, slimy pond. She loved it all.

The following week's teaching covered 'Child Development' – affirmations that children should receive at different ages to develop healthily. By the time Gail finished this and the 'Structure of

Intelligence' Assessment she felt completely drained. She found the teaching covering the necessity to grieve over lost things in childhood and the accompanying role play very hard to cope with. She was really scared at the intensity of what she felt but God gave her Psalm 34: *'I sought the Lord, and he answered me; he delivered me from all my fears.'* She realised she needed to grieve for some of the losses in her life. For the mother she had never known, and things that had happened through working in Mozambique. She grieved for some of the kids, and her friendships with Angus, Martin, Thomas and Richmond, as well as the personal things that had been stolen.

Thanksgiving was enjoyed by everyone. It was fun having to get dressed up, and eating turkey and stuffing, and pumpkin pie, amongst beautiful decorations and lots of balloons.

The following week teaching covered 'Child Abuse'. Gail was anxious that she would be shocked and not know how to cope with what she heard. She was! She spent a lot of time feeling sad, angry and frustrated, realising the street kids in Mozambique suffered every single kind of abuse. She also realised it was not the United States of America where one could call the police, social welfare, or a therapist. She spent a lot of time crying, or being too stunned to do anything.

The worst was the Satanic Ritual Abuse. Two of Gail's friends had to work through their own first-hand knowledge of this. Gail felt totally inadequate; she felt their pain, and understood the long-lasting effects childhood abuse had on people, and realised again how very important this teaching was for her to grasp. Gail received bad news from Beira this same week. One of the skids had been run over and was in traction in hospital, another had nearly drowned, and another had broken into the office and stolen her radio/tape deck and some money and had not been seen since. Gail cried, not for the loss of her things, but because the kid who took them would be afraid of punishment and so would probably leave Beira. She would lose the opportunity to tell him about Jesus. That made her cry.

As Gail learned about Multiple Personality Disorder she knew it was the problem with one of her boys, and realised there was no one able to help him. She wondered how many others there were like him, in Mozambique, mentally 'freaked out' after all the trauma they had been through. It made her feel desolate and without hope for the nation, but as she and Anna prayed together, she realised afresh that she did not have to carry all the responsibilities herself. Her prayer was that God would send people to Mozambique who could help those who had been through so much, and for an effective way to stop the abuse and suffering.

To break the tension of the week there was a lot of fun too. Gail got totally soaked with a two gallon super soaker; she and Polly got into throwing grapes during dinner, and Polly ended up squashing grapes into Gail's ears. Jani put salt in Gail's coffee, June shoved a banana in her face, which ended up down June's back and in Jani's hair; Debbie picked up Gail's 'cracker' pen and it exploded in the middle of one of the lectures and two people had birthdays celebrated with musical statues, pass the parcel, balloons, lollipops and funny hats. One Saturday Gail and three others volunteered to sweep the roof of the lodge which was scary to begin with but ended up with a of fun, noise and, of course, dirt.

As the temperatures began to drop, and autumn

turned the trees yellow, red, orange and brown, Gail wrote this poem summarising recent teaching:

A heart that is broken, crying, sad and lonely
Not knowing how to hide the pain
Longing for wholeness
Yearning for justice,
  or to forget the guilt, the shame.

Where are the shoulders to cry on?
Where are the arms to hold me?
Where are the ears that allow me to speak?
When will this darkness end?
  and the tears stop running
  falling down my face in the hidden hours.

Why the anguish? Why the hatred?
Why the desolation of fear?
Is there a way out of here?
Can I escape the nightmare?
Is there any hope left in this world for me?

I only know of one
His hope is the anchor of my soul!

Gail read a book on grief for her third book report. It upset her because it questioned 'Why?' Why did God allow a person to die? She was looking for some answers she could share with others.

Half-way through the course, one week covered substance abuse. A lot of heavy teaching, lightened somewhat when they moved onto the topic of dreams. Gail could never remember what she dreamed, which she thought was rather a shame, but Gleide dreamt that Gail got married and had a **big** party!

As the teaching covered roles played in a family living with substance abuse, Gail had to work out roles played in her own family, and answer questions like 'What do I like about myself?', 'Who has ever made me feel loved, accepted, worthwhile?', 'How have they done that?' and to the question 'Who has ever made me feel defective, inadequate, or "I don't measure up"?' she wrote, 'Mainly myself by not believing I'm worth liking and by comparing myself to other more outgoing and gifted people. Occasionally by school mates – that I wasn't one of the "gang". I withdraw and I don't talk about myself, or share my thoughts and feelings. I pretend to be strong, independent, and "OK", self-sufficient.' Her constant prayer was 'Change my heart and make me new and secure in the Lord.'

Angels and mortals week was special. Everyone picked a fellow student to whom they would be a secret angel. Gail received encouragement, and little gifts from her 'angel', and a 'letter from her "Heavenly Father"' which read:

'Gail, As an angel of the Lord Most High, I have been commissioned to share the following.

"You are so special to me! No words can begin to explain the joy I feel when you draw near to me! For it is only when my heart can minister directly into your heart, that you can catch a glimpse of how proud I am of my precious daughter. I truly long to just hold you in my arms and shower my love on to you. All you need do is open yourself completely to receive my gifts. I have placed a very special anointing on you for my work. I will lead you in this so just **go for it**! You are special! Love, Your Heavenly Father"'

On Friday, round the fireplace, with orange juice and Danish pastries, all was revealed. Cristal, you made a great angel.

Ellen and Polly were baptised in a hot tub one evening, along with much joy, fun and food. Gleide left to return to Brazil and donated some items of clothing to Gail's wardrobe, and John, ex-Mozambique, telephoned from USA. To round off a relaxed interval, Gail found that the Bible and pens she had left in the classroom had been hijacked and a ransom note read, 'If you want your Bible and pens back you must say "Purple Baboons sat on yellow Bananas and squashed them" loudly during announcements at supper tonight, or else!'

Halloween, the high point of the Satanist calendar, bought back bad memories for some students, and generated much prayer for the children destined for sacrifice. It made Gail feel sick, and she wished the Christian church was more committed to doing battle against the kingdom of darkness.

Shame and self-esteem teaching was heavy, under-lining four basic things everyone should know in order to be healthy:

- I am lovable.
- I am valuable.
- I am capable.
- I am forgivable.

It looked at countries that were shame-based, shown in their particular brand of humour, sarcasm, or cultural prejudices. To lift her spirits, Gail woke next morning to find it had snowed. She loved snow.

Gail joined a crowd of students for some five-pin bowling in Winfield which was fun, and a new experience for her. She also made a contract with herself to get to bed by 10.30 pm and up early enough to go for a walk before breakfast each day. Her time in Canada was running out and she wanted to make the most of it.

A number of mentally handicapped people from Joy Christian Fellowship came to stay. Throughout the week the CIN students assumed different roles to help them understand the difficulties handicapped people lived with. Gail's role was 'in a wheel chair with cerebral palsy, able to move only a couple of steps at a time, speak with difficulty, and got grumpy when tired'. Afterwards she wrote her imagined experiences: that people laughed at her when she tried to feed herself and made a mess, they were impatient and tried to feed her. They asked lots of questions and didn't give her time to answer, before asking another. They found it hard to listen patiently to what she had to say, and left as soon as they could. Most people assumed she had nothing to say. It made her feel like she was bothering people, and she didn't feel like talking to anyone because they didn't want to listen! This role play was recorded on a video tape she bought back from Canada and showed her to be a remarkably good actress.

She did a Bible study with several of these special visitors on the fruit produced when abiding in the vine. They made a visual aid together hanging different fruit on a tree branch. Gail learned much about gentleness and unconditional love from them, and found it a humbling experience being with them.

Gail was coming to terms with many emotional and practical situations, past and present, and was under a lot of pressure and stress. At the same time she was trying to decide how to see everyone and do everything she planned in three short weeks in England and Europe on the way home at the end of the course.

She welcomed the chance to join a group of students travelling to Banff for a weekend. She loved the beautiful mountain scenery and snow. It was very cold (−30°C) during the night, but the hotel sauna and hot tub came in handy. A visit to the Upper Hot Springs was great fun, sitting in the warm water with falling snow freezing the hair. After washing in the showers, hair froze again walking to the vehicle.

The following week one of Gail's friends had to leave the course, and she recorded in her journal:

I climbed into my Father's heart to see what I would
*   see . . .*
It was warm and soft and comfortable . . . just room
*   enough for me.*

I felt His love around me, I felt His warm embrace
I felt His care and tenderness, as He gently touched
*   my face!*

I sensed His muscles rippling, I could feel His mighty
*   power*
I knew He would protect me and save me in each
*   hour.*

There was a shining brightness of purity and light
It shone into my heart as well, and chased away the
*   night.*

I entered deeper and further in, I couldn't find the
*   end*
of all the goodness He'd planned for me, because I
*   am His friend.*

One student said Gail reminded her of Melody Green, and that God would use her as He had used Melody – to mother others, and to reach out to thousands of people. That she would be a comfort not only to the street kids and those around her, but to many others too. Gail's 'angel' friend Cristal wrote this to her:

'I'm Special

"I'm special. In all the world there's nobody like me.
Since the beginning of time, there has never been

another person like me. Nobody has my smile. Nobody has my eyes, my nose, my hair, my voice. I'm special.

No one can be found who has my handwriting. Nobody anywhere has my tastes – for food or music or art. No one sees things just as I do.

In all of time there's been no one who laughs like me, no one who cries like me. And what makes me laugh and cry will never provoke identical laughter and tears from anybody else, ever.

No one reacts to any situation just as I would react. I'm special.

I'm the only one in all of creation who has my set of abilities. Oh, there will always be somebody who is better at one of the things I'm good at, but no one in the universe can reach the quality of my combination of talents, ideas, abilities and feelings. Like a room full of instruments, some may excel alone, but none can match the symphony sound when all are played together. I'm a symphony.

Through all of eternity no one will ever look, talk, walk, think or do like me. I'm special. I'm rare. And in rarity there is great value.

Because of my great rare value, I need not attempt to imitate others. I will accept – yes, celebrate – my differences.

I'm special. And I'm beginning to realise it's no accident that I'm special. I'm beginning to see that God made me special for a very special purpose. He has a job for me that no one else can do as well as I can. Out of all the billions God has created only I can do what He has planned for me, only I can love and serve Him in my uniqueness.

I'm special.

I am a part of God that He has placed only in me.

He has made me special!"'

She finished the page with this:

*'Gail, I pray God will show you just how special you truly are to Him! May this be a very real revelation to your heart, soul and whole being. God just simply, but so deeply wants you to know "**you are loved**!"'*

Thank you Cristal. Everyone, everywhere needs to know that too.

For her final project Gail designed a pamphlet presenting the story of one of the Beira street kids, entitled 'Who am I?' When the dreaded presentation day finally arrived, she tried to dress up a bit like a street kid and sang a song – and people seemed to enjoy it. She was so impressed by everyone else and the variety and originality of their projects, she wasn't sure she had done very well with hers. She need not have worried. A fellow student, Val, was so impressed with her leaflet that she suggested it be printed and distributed worldwide 'to help people really identify with street children – and in turn help the children themselves – thus bearing much fruit.'

It was cold and snowy, as Gail prepared to wear a dress and new, shorter hairstyle, for graduation on 9th December, celebrated afterwards by delicious chicken and cheese-cake. During the evening, Gail discussed with the school leaders the possibility of doing her practicum in Mozambique, and the need for some modification for Africa. It would mean keeping a journal for six months, recording therapy with individual street kids and classes in the Casa Ré-om school, and setting up interpersonal team support. She was asked if she could be available as a member of staff for a Children In Need course in Europe, because of her practical experience in Mozambique, to which she readily agreed. Certificates were handed out, each person was prayed for and received presents from the $1 shop. It was special but it was also a sad time saying goodbye to everyone.

From Vancouver Gail flew to Toronto, Montreal, Lisbon and eventually to London. She wrote this at 00:30 am at Lisbon Airport, 3rd December, 1993:

Why,
  When I know that I need you so much
Why,
  When I know that I live by your touch
Do I forget to come to you
  Do I busy myself with others, and myself,
and I forget you,
  and think I don't need you.

This year I choose to be
  a seeker of wisdom and understanding
a diligent seeker
  not complacent
not waiting for it to fall from the sky
  but seeking, earnestly
praying fervently
  drawing near, consciously
longing, deeply and passionately
  to know your heart

to hear your voice
  to be one with you
a worshipper, in spirit and in truth.

To walk in your light
  To let your word be my guide
No compromise, only passion
  love and surrender
obedience and courage – to know and walk
  in truth and humility.

She also wrote down her personal goals for 1994, amongst which were:

- More self-definition and boundaries – love of self and fear of the Lord
- Deeper in worship/song-writing/prophecy
- Do fun/crazy things – laugh a lot
- Fall in love and give of myself willingly to the man of God's choice
- Be vulnerable and open as much as I can
- **Live abundantly** – work hard, play hard, be a friend, do new and exciting things **seek God!**
- Have needs, be **weak**.

Gail had a busy time seeing friends in London, and travelling with Thomas in Germany and Switzerland over Christmas, and eventually arrived home, in time to rest for a couple of days before the regional YWAM staff conference, preparing to return to Mozambique at the end of January, and start learning Sena, the local dialect used in and around Beira.

O Jesus - what a wonder you are
    You are so beautiful,
        So majestic
            so full of life !!

I can see you all around
    hear you in the songs of the birds
        feel you in the breath of clean air

Your creation - it really does tell of
    your glory
        More than words could ever say

    So perfect
        So natural
            So alive and new,
                and exciting

What a priviledge
    to be a child of God
        to know you - the Creator
            to walk with you - the author of life
                our hope,
                    our refuge,
                        our rock,
                            our Eternal God & Father
                                You are - 1 Am

Chapter 12

The Wedding

'Mum, John asked me to marry him and I said "Yes"!'

For once the telephone line from Mozambique was clear, and I could hear the excitement and shyness mixed together in Gail's voice.

'Wow! Fantastic!'

'We're going to telephone tonight so John can speak to Dad,' she continued, 'so please make sure he's there.'

Wendy had been staying with us the week before this telephone call. We had just received a letter from Gail telling us about an American called John Wickes, who rode a mountain bike and wore tie-dyed T-shirts. We did not want to pump Wendy for details, but she did say things could get serious, that John and Gail were taking things very slowly, and that John was a nice person. Now this phone call. Slow my foot!

Gail met John when she got back to Beira at the end of January 1994, at the English-speaking Sunday evening service. Throughout the service John saw two beautiful eyes glancing at him across the crowded room. He saw golden brown hair, above a huge smile, and he 'felt' her joy, peace and personality. Towards the end of the meeting the preacher numbered every-one off to form small groups and John tried hard not to panic when he realised Gail would be in his group. Trying not to look at her, John found they had the same opinions on the questions discussed.

During the following week, Gail threw all her mother's careful teaching out the window, and tele-phoned John every day. It was probably good that she was 'forward' because John admitted that he was not one to initiate relationships.

The next Sunday there were plenty of vacant seats, but Gail chose to sit on the floor at John's feet, which unnerved him somewhat and the Bible story of Ruth and Boaz flashed through his mind. Several weeks before this, John had promised that the day rain stopped him working on the Africa Inland Mission Bible School he would pop in to hang doors at Casa Ré-om. It was amazing how often it rained in the next few weeks.

Following on from her training in Canada, Gail started to set up a counselling programme for the children. She felt strongly that she needed to com-plete the practicum, although she realised it was an enormous undertaking. Angola was often in her mind and she spent a lot of time praying for the children affected by the war there, although Gail never actu-ally 'saw' beyond Mozambique, joking that it was for life. She said it worried her a bit, but perhaps it was so she could be free to follow her husband's vision!

By 15th February Gail wrote in her diary:

'Spoke to John on the phone tonight – made a feeble excuse to phone him – haven't seen him since Sunday night and was missing him – can you believe it? He seemed really happy that I'd called – we chatted for half an hour ... Invited me for lunch or dinner sometime. Felt like I'd burst – stupid grin all over my face – went and confessed to Wend that I think I'm in love ... her advice – relax and enjoy it! **Freak out!** I don't remember feeling this passionate about anyone – not to the extent that I make the first move! **What is God doing in me?** My pride is out the window. I'm trying to not be influenced by my "romantic environment" i.e. Debs and Wend (both engaged to be married). What will Mom think? This is the first guy I've wanted to write home about ... weird ... scarey ... I **hope** he is feeling the same and that it's God doing this in us!'

Their friendship progressed, and on 8th March John showed Gail a list of 50 dating suggestions for married couples he had found. The next Tuesday she found a note under her pillow:

'#32 I hope you enjoy it as much as I did! John'

Her sheets were sprinkled with talcum powder, and Date #32 said:

'– perfume the sheets.'

Gail's comment, 'He's crazy.'

That was the night she decided to write home and tell us about John.

As she and John walked to the 'ship's graveyard' not far from Casa Ré-om one day, Gail talked about a vocational training project for the street kids. Excitedly John shared how God had given him exactly the same vision seven years ago, before he left America.

He felt he knew now, altogether, why he had come to Africa.

Having had a broken engagement, John worried about faithfulness in their relationship, but soon decided Gail was the perfect person for him. Their attitudes, likes, expectations, desires and goals were so similar. He saw loyalty, dedication, steadfastness and perseverance in her. In everything she did, her goal was to do things right. John admits he's just a big kid, and sometimes people didn't know whether to laugh with them, or give them a wide berth, but John and Gail had the same zany sense of humour and they knew how to have fun together. After knowing Gail for two weeks, John caught himself thinking of marriage. He wrestled and prayed about this until Sunday 6th March, and, with a feeling of great peace, decided he would propose to Gail on the following Friday, 11th March. This would be the first day of the first month of the Jewish Calendar which John considered sufficiently auspicious for the occasion.

That Friday there was a birthday party in Dondo, 45 minutes drive inland from Beira. The celebration ended too late to catch a bus back to Beira, so six of them flagged down a lorry, and climbed on the back. It was full of sacks of rice, and a number of goats tied together. John and Gail sat on a sack in one corner, the others packing themselves in as best they could. John asked Gail if she had made any new year resolutions, and she said no, but she had made a prayer request. At that moment the goats decided to move. Some backwards, some forwards and others sideways, butting, pushing, and standing on any toes that happened to get in the way. John hung his head in defeat, and then looking up at the moonless, cloudless, beautiful night sky, decided to try again.

'What was your prayer request?'

'To fall in love!'

John felt things were improving, and when Gail asked

'What about you?' he said

'I'd like to spend the rest of my life with you,' and without missing a beat she said

'I could live with that.' She replied so quickly, John thought she might have misunderstood him, so he said

'I'd like to marry you this year', and Gail immediately responded

'It'll have to be before October because Debs is leaving then.'

All John could think of was 'Wow. That was easy!'

As they went for a walk next evening, Gail asked John to call and talk to her Dad. He said 'Sure, when do you want to call,' and she replied, 'In about half an hour.' She increased John's panic by mentioning that her father might make it a bit rough for him, but he'd just be playing.

John never actually asked permission to marry Gail. Rikki asked him if he liked ice-cream, and he said 'Yes.' 'You'll get along well in this family then. Do you love Gail more than ice-cream?' John responded 'Yes' and that was that.

One day when Gail and John met, Gail was upset. She was hurting for her parents planning a wedding for her to marry someone they had not met. John immediately made arrangements to travel from Mozambique to meet his ice-cream eating future family. On the way he had a very strong impression that God was saying 'This is your family now' and we enjoyed an excellent weekend together. He told us he had inscribed the date they got engaged in cement at the top of the Bible School roof the morning of the day he proposed to Gail – you could call that 'blind faith', but it proves he was sure of himself, and what Gail's response would be.

Walking along the beach one day Gail said to John that if anything ever happened to her, she wanted him to throw her ashes in the sea. It seemed such a strange thing for a healthy, happy, in love 28-year-old to say at the time.

John struggled with a number of issues. Would he have enough money to meet their needs? Would Gail become an American? Or he a Zimbabwean? As John considered these things God gave him peace. For Gail too there seemed a lot of issues God was not answering, but she believed He had a plan. For both of them it seemed God was saying 'Rejoice. Trust in me with all your hearts and lean not to your own understanding.'

We were in Beira for Debbie's official engagement to Elias, when Wendy got Gail and John onto the beach one evening for a photo session. It was wonderful to be there to share their happiness, and enjoy the fun and nonsense those photographs created. Two weeks later John and Gail came home for ten days to start wedding preparations. Four of the photographs Wendy took were selected for wedding notifications which were posted to friends and relations around the world who were unlikely to come to the wedding. In this way John's friends could see what Gail looked like, and Gail's friends saw who she was marrying. The invitations were designed and printed on computer, and assembled and addressed by the whole family.

Gail's dress design and material were lovingly put together exactly as she had dreamed they would be.

Debbie, and Gail's sisters Lindsay and Carol, were happy with their blue floral bridesmaid dresses; shoes were found; flowers were planned; Gail selected a gift list at a store in town; John found just the right shirts and waistcoats for himself and his three groomsmen; the menu, venue and caterer for the reception were confirmed. It was amazing how much was achieved in a short time, and there was very little left to organise by the time they returned to Beira.

Two weeks before the wedding Casa Ré-om was packed for a 'Wedding Blessing'. Pastor Bonga was a particularly happy man. He had always worried about Gail's spinster status. Many Mozambicans stood up during the service to say what a blessing Gail had been to them. There were so many who wanted to speak they had to be stopped, or the event would have gone on for many hours.

The weekend before the wedding, John, Gail, Rikki and I were invited to Sanyati Baptist Mission in the midland region of Zimbabwe, where John's mother had just completed a two-year nursing commitment before finally retiring from the mission field at the age of 71. These lovely Southern Baptist missionaries organised a delightful American bridal shower, and were very generous and hospitable to all of us. Not to be left out, the Southern Baptist mission ladies living in Harare prepared a lovely lunch in Gail's honour, and Missy Moses spent hours making beautiful sugar flowers which decorated the wedding cake. In fact those flowers decorated three wedding cakes – Gail and John's, Debbie and Elias' in Beira, and then Wendy took them with her to England when she married Jim.

We parked two caravans and a camp-a-van in the front garden to accommodate the extra people staying with us for the wedding. My brother came from Cape Town, Gail's maternal grandmother travelled from Johannesburg, Rikki's mother, brother and sister drove from Durban, South Africa, and Wendy, Debbie and Elias, were the first to come from Mozambique. As a surprise for Gail, Joan Parsons decided at the eleventh hour to fly from England for the wedding, and Helen and her husband Mark and small son, travelled from Mozambique. Not only did Joan have a joyful reunion with the Decker family, but with her own as well.

Gary and Chris Atkins and two short-term volunteers brought the 10 street kids living in the Casa Ré-om centre from Beira by 'chicken bus', the basic form of transport throughout Africa, and they were accommodated at the Christian Retreat 'Resthaven' where the wedding reception was to be held. On Thursday afternoon before the wedding, Gail had the 'skids' at the local shopping mall to buy them tennis shoes. While negotiating a busy main road 12-year-old Simao was reprimanded for dangerously dawdling. He flew into a rage and ran away. The rest of the group returned to the house, and when Gail went back to look for him, Simao had disappeared. We spent an anxious night wondering where he was, and praying for his safety. Wearing only a T-shirt and shorts we knew he would be cold, and hungry, streetwise or not. He could speak some Shona, the local African language, and we realised he could get to anywhere in Zimbabwe if he so wished. The Police could not accept a missing person report for 24 hours. All we could do was pray.

On Friday afternoon Gail and Wendy were delayed, at a dressmaker, for an hour and a half in the centre of Harare, and as they drove out along one of the major thoroughfares, Wendy saw Simao crossing the road right in front of them. Picking him up, he showed some relief, but refused to say anything. When Gail drove triumphantly up the drive with Simao we nearly hugged him with relief. He refused to say anything for several hours, but finally told Gary what had happened, and apologised to Gail. He reached the centre of Harare, somehow, and was picked up by the Police on suspicion of stealing the tennis shoes he had under his arm in their box. The Police kept him in custody for the night and released him on Friday morning. He said he was on his way back to Resthaven, 30km away, when Gail picked him up. Did God orchestrate the delay in town to coincide with Simao crossing a busy main road in the heart of the city?

The wedding rehearsal went according to plan on Friday evening, except for Simao, who, by way of punishment was not allowed to participate. 20 people came back to the house for a curry supper, followed by a time of sharing, laughter and giving of gifts. Gail gave John's Mum, Betty, a seed opal for her wedding band. Her ring had spaces for 12 stones, her own, her late husband's, and each of her five children and their spouses. The opal was to fill the last space waiting for John's bride.

Many friends laboured lovingly and ingeniously to make patches for a friendship quilt which had been sewn into a double bed cover. This, together with a photograph album covered with material left over from Gail's wedding dress, with the photographs from the Sanyati Mission bridal shower inside, were un-wrapped and admired. A heart shaped ice-cream cake deliciously ended the evening.

Saturday began with hair appointments, and later,

amongst the confusion of photographers and bouquets arriving Gail received a telephone call from Mike Oman in Ireland. Ten o'clock, with the wedding service due to begin in half an hour everyone was waiting for the bride to get dressed, but Gail was working to African time and was unconcerned about the clock ticking on, wringing every last ounce of enjoyment from each moment. After many photographs, and video footage Gail was at last on her way to the church, looking stunning in cream satin, the bodice and elbow length sleeves overlaid with lace and seed pearls, a wreath of fresh flowers and blue ribbon in her hair, and carrying a simple sheaf of champagne coloured roses.

Guests had been singing praise songs in the church and the atmosphere was one of joy and expectation. Our clown team did a wonderful job ushering and handing out order of service sheets proclaiming Revelation 19:7, *'Let us rejoice and be glad, and give the glory to Him.'* Guests walked into the church under a banner especially made by all the children in the school in Beira.

The bridal procession was led in by Pastor Bonga and his wife, from Beira, and Baba Tsuma, from Sanyati Mission blowing a kudu horn, followed by Elias and the street children singing and dancing. Rikki and Gail walked some distance behind, with Debbie, Lindsay and Carol following. Gail was radiant, greeting various friends as she slowly walked up the aisle.

Con Heyns, head of YWAM Zimbabwe, commenced the service. There was more praise and worship, readings from Ecclesiastes 4:9–12, in English and Portuguese, and together Rikki and I gave Gail to John. John then interrupted the service to present the 'lobola' or traditional African 'bride price' to us. We knew nothing of this plan. The clowns brought 2 goats, 2 ducks and 2 chickens into the front of the church! Everyone roared with laughter and clapped with delight as Rikki 'accepted' the gift. They were then removed outside again, and subsequently returned to the farm from whence they came.

Gail and John exchanged vows which they had written themselves, Gail's including Ruth's beautiful commitment to her mother-in-law Naomi from Ruth 1:16. Rikki spoke briefly about the importance of team work in a marriage, the need for good management,

co- operation, and working together. He then covered
John and Gail with a Jewish talit or prayer shawl,
signifying the transference of his fatherly authority
over Gail to John as her husband. John loves all
things Jewish and this bought a very special dimen-
sion to the service as their friends gathered round to
pray for them. As John and Gail took communion
together, Noemia from Brazil, married to a Dondo
pastor, played her guitar and sang in Portuguese, her

magnificent voice filling the building. As Gail and John signed the register at the front of the church, Trish Mbanga danced to an unusual song called *In the Garden*, inspired by the original beauty of the garden of Eden, and the purity of Adam and Eve.

The boys from Beira held praise banners, proclaiming the names of God, in an archway as the wedding party moved towards tables laden with fruit punch and chocolate cake, and John and Gail cut their wedding cake. There must have been at least 350 people who rejoiced with us at the church.

Simao was heartbroken at not being allowed to take part in the wedding, and ran away again, just before Gail arrived at the church. One of the volunteers followed him as he ran for an hour, without stopping – a remarkable feat for a 12-year-old. He finally lay down and slept by the side of the road for half an hour, and was persuaded to return to the church. By then everyone was at the reception, and it was mid-afternoon before they reached Resthaven.

More photographs were taken in the beautiful garden of some friends, and Gail and John visited with the husband, paralysed with cancer, before driving to Resthaven at noon, where the reception tables, decorated with white and yellow cloths, and yellow flowers and ribbons, were spread under ancient shade trees. 200 guests enjoyed the lighthearted speeches and the cold buffet lunch in what one described as a 'Garden of Eden' setting. John ran into a cross-cultural problem during the reception. In America the bride and groom leave the reception before any of the guests. In Zimbabwe the couple take time to visit each table and talk to all the guests even if some have to leave before they do. Gail and John finally left at half past three, riding an elderly tandem

161

bicycle. Gail was laughing so much John had to do most of the work to get it up the hill and around the corner, where our 1968 Datsun 1600 proclaiming 'Just Married' across the back, reinforced by many clanking tin cans tied behind, waited, out of sight of the remaining guests. John and Gail drove to Nyanga, part of the eastern border mountains of Zimbabwe, while John's mother Betty prepared to fly to the United States of America that night. Lindsay set off with a friend for a year-long overseas working holiday a week later.

John and Gail stayed in an hotel for four nights and spent their days relaxing, climbing the surrounding hills and enjoying the beautiful views. Gail teased John every mealtime about his American eating habits, and was particularly delighted when he ordered chicken, watching his face as he realised he would be expected to eat it with a knife and fork, and not with his fingers. His comment – 'I've never eaten chicken with a knife and fork in my life.'

From this idyllic time they joined a 'Share the Cup' Mozambique Missionary conference at nearby Rhodes Nyanga cottages. Everyone thought they were quite mad to spend part of their honeymoon there, although it was a refreshing time of teaching, discussions, prayer and visiting with friends from all over Mozambique – some of whom Gail hardly ever saw. One day, when their YWAM colleagues from Beira were praying for Gail and John, Gail got a very clear vision of travelling along a road. There were some rocky places but these were negotiated, as was a hill, and on the other side lay a wide river. On one side of the road leading to the river there was beautiful lush flowering vegetation, on the other side it was arid desert with nothing there at all. Gail had a sensation of moving forward together with John, and she knew she crossed the river. At the same time, John felt such a deep grief overwhelm him that it was all he could do not to break down completely. They shared these experiences with each other afterwards but did not understand them.

A week after their wedding they returned to Harare, arriving at eight o'clock Sunday night. John was keen to open their wedding presents right away, and as he carried the first pile from their bedroom to the lounge, he felt very specifically that they should open all of them, and we shared their enjoyment until late.

Next morning they did some shopping and packed the car to its limits with camping gear, before setting off for Mana Pools, a National Parks wildlife area on the banks of the Zambezi River. As Gail opened the gate, I hugged John and said: 'Take good care of your wife.' Gail and John had both been to Mana at different times, and Gail's comment to her friend Viv after her visit had been 'If heaven is anything like Mana, I want to be there.'

True love ......
       dying
            to yourself.

It hurts.
    Am I ready?
       Am I willing?
Is this what you want, God.
Do I need to be committed
      to church?
         to a group?
           to a person?

" I have this against you....
     you have lost your first love
       you have lost your zeal
         your newness
            your "life" "

In quietness & confidence —
    waiting,
      trusting,
        resting in you —
shall be my strength.

    Amen and Amen

Chapter 13

From Glory to Glory

TOOT, TOOT, TOOT, TOOT, TOOT, TOOT, TOOT!
Nine-thirty on Sunday night, 29th May I had been
asleep for half an hour when the car hooting at the
gate woke me. I thought 'Gail and John have decided
to come back early, and don't have a key to get in.'
Rikki still in his overalls from fixing a car, went to the
gate. The next thing I knew he opened the bedroom
door, asked if I was awake, and came round the bed
sobbing, saying the unthinkable:

'Gail has been killed by a buffalo at Mana.'

I said, 'Oh my darling, I'm so sorry, I'm so sorry'.
My heart went out to Rikki as he buried his face in my
shoulder, and we clung to one another. Then I
thought about John, but Rikki said he was apparently
alright.

Realising we had people waiting in the house, I
threw on dressing gown and slippers. There was a
dream-like quality walking down the brightly lit
passage, having to move, but not wanting to, to meet
our good friend Ken Jenkins, and Missy Moses and her
husband. The Police at Chirundu on the Zambezi
River had contacted the Moses' because our telephone

was out of order. Missy had answered the telephone, and deeply shocked, had to ask the policeman to repeat everything twice, and then cried: 'Do I have to go and tell them?' They contacted Ken, an Elder in our sister church, who agreed to come with them to give us the news. All three were very shaken, as Rikki and I struggled to comprehend their news. It was hard to believe, but so much harder for them to come and tell us.

We agreed not to contact anyone else that night – it seemed pointless to disturb a good night's sleep, and then we prayed together.

After they prayed for us, and John, we prayed that God's Kingdom would gain much fruit from this tragedy – otherwise it didn't make any sense at all. They left, surely doubting our assurances that we would be fine – we just felt numb.

Rikki and I sat down close together in silence, and then the tears came. Rikki voiced his anger at the thought that Gail and John had not realised the dangers of close contact with animals in the wild, but I felt deep down they had done nothing foolish to cause this accident. We discussed what needed to be done next day and went to bed with a deep concern for John – Where was he? Was he on his own? Was he really alright?

Next morning we broke the news to Carol and my mother, Ruth, and our domestic staff. More tears, more sharing, more disbelief, and lots of loving one another. Rikki went to his office with a long list of people to telephone. It was a difficult and exhausting morning for him, but meanwhile our faulty telephone was repaired and we felt more in contact with the world.

Arrangements to bring Gail back to Harare were

taken out of our hands by a mortician who grew up a close neighbour and friend to Gail, and we were told to expect John sometime Monday evening. Dr Paul Boone, one of John's groomsmen drove with his wife Carol from Sanyati Mission Hospital to Karoi, a five-hour journey, to meet John there and help him with necessary documentation, and the two Christian doctors who had been camping next to John and Gail completed a three vehicle convoy which bought John safely home. The latter had stayed with him throughout the ordeal, and we were so grateful.

They assured us that no medical equipment or expertise in the world could have made any difference to Gail, and they had done all that was humanly possible. It was comforting to know this and we thanked them for their kindness, love and care.

As soon as we were sitting down with mugs of coffee, John said 'Do you want me to tell you what happened?' and we said we would like to hear, if he felt able to tell us. 'Yes,' he said, 'I want to tell you. I've told it all several times already, to the police and so on.'

John and Gail had spent the week in the Mana Pools campsite on the banks of the Zambezi River in John's light-weight two-man tent, walking out game viewing several hours each day, and spending time writing wedding gift thank you letters. On their last evening, an elephant had followed them as they returned to camp, and they were watching him carefully until he lost interest in them and began browsing a tree. They stopped, in knee-high grass, when they saw some grass stalks move at one side of the path. They spent several minutes chatting, and watching, and laughed when four or five small birds flew up. John stepped down a dip in the path to see round a bend, and realised they were on the edge of a gully with such long grass that it would not be safe to continue that way.

As he did so, he saw a big, old, bull buffalo standing an arm's length away, and called a warning to Gail. As he turned away to the right he moved out of the buffalo's range of vision, and as Gail wheeled to the left above John on the path the animal charged, impacting Gail on her right buttock, and tossing her several metres into long grass. He continued his charge, despite John's frantic yells to distract him, and then backed off far enough for John to reach Gail. Meanwhile John's shouts alerted the office personnel who arrived with guns and a stretcher, and shot the animal before it could charge again. Gail was lying in a foetal position and John realised she was badly injured. He tried resuscitation, but did not want to move her too much. He said, 'Gail, don't leave me, but if you've already got a glimpse of heaven then it's OK to go.' He said he realised in that moment he would be so mad if he was in a similar situation and someone prayed for him to come back! Even through this incredible experience John felt an urge to 'Rejoice' in his heart, just as God had been telling him from the beginning of the year. With hindsight, we believe the sigh Gail gave as John went towards her was her spirit leaving her body, bound for heaven and her Lord. When the doctors examined her they found extensive bruising on her left side – John had suspected serious internal injuries – but she also had a broken neck.

When John finished, he said 'I'm sorry, I'm so sorry,' and I asked him why he was apologising to us. 'Because I thought you'd blame me for what has happened' he said.

'No Way!'

Rikki had been that route before, and we were not
about to repeat history. We assured John we had
given Gail to God when she was little, as we had with
Lindsay, Carol and little Bradley, and we had given
her to John with great joy. He was our son, and
nothing would ever change that. He visibly relaxed
as we took that burden from him.

The news travelled fast, and we began receiving visits, cards, letters, telephone calls, flowers and meals from hundreds of people. John's mother flew back from America to be with us for two weeks, missing her granddaughter's wedding, but it was so good to have her share all the love and support we received, and for her to be with John. We felt God's strength through all the prayers of concerned and loving people.

People continued in a constant stream, bringing their comfort and expressions of love and support. By the Wednesday morning I was tired, and the emotional dam broke, as I walked back and forth in the privacy of our back garden. I cried for over an hour, repeating: 'My beautiful Gail. Why God, tell me why!' and when I had cried it all out God answered very quietly and clearly:

'Because she has endured enough for me, and I love her.'

Then, sitting quietly in God's beautiful creation, I realised His ultimate gift to Gail was John's love and two perfect weeks of marriage and companionship. I had to accept God knew what He was doing. Having worked in a medical rehabilitation centre, I could also accept God's goodness in not leaving Gail a quadriplegic, with the pain, frustration and readjustment involved, or for John to be tied to an invalid for the rest of his life. The fact that Gail's neck was broken was a great help to me in being able to accept her death, and to continue to know God's love.

Rikki was having problems of his own. He didn't have time to mourn his first wife Elspeth's death, with a two-month-old baby to look after, and when Gail came back from Canada she pointed out that Rikki's workaholism was masking that grief. I had always known this, but Gail, with her new knowledge and youthful enthusiasm, said it had to be dealt with. Easier said than done. And now, four short months later, her own death provided the way. Rikki had to work through grieving for Gail, and in doing so, it opened up things he had thought long buried, and he grieved for Elspeth too – a double dose. Tried in that kind of fire, he has come out purer gold, and the proof has been seen in a more relaxed and restful person, who will even take time out to fly kites occasionally.

On Thursday morning, Trish, who had danced at the end of the wedding service, came and danced for us again. It was a memorable interlude, sitting in the sunshine and watching her, as she interpreted Michael Card's *Simeon's Song* for us. The words 'Now let your servant depart in peace' were especially meaningful to us – Simeon's work on earth had come to an end, and so had Gail's.

John asked me to make a wreath of fresh flowers similar to the one Gail had worn on her wedding day, and that evening, together with John's mother, newly arrived from America, went to say goodbye to Gail in the funeral home chapel. John put the wreath on her head as she lay in the coffin. He hoped this visit would help him – his last memory of seeing her as she had been at the Mana Pools camp was not a happy one – but it did not. It did help me, however. I touched her cheek, which felt like marble, and said:

'Goodbye Gaily girl. You gave so much happiness to so many.'

On Friday 3rd June, at 9.00 in the morning, we had a simple service at the Crematorium, taken by Angus, our Youth Pastor. We have never seen the chapel so full, and it was good to greet friends afterwards, sharing the strength we felt, with them. At 10.30 we had a Thanksgiving Service for Gail's life at Greystone Park Fellowship, and over 500 people were there.

It was a wonderful service with all the beautiful praise banners round the walls, as they had been during the wedding, and the flower arrangements we had received grouped on either side at the front of the church. We sang songs of praise, thanksgiving and worship, rejoicing in our loving God.

John was the first to speak. He told how, from the beginning of the year, God had been telling him to 'Rejoice and Celebrate'. The morning of the day Gail was killed he had been reading in his Bible the account of Nehemiah when the people were in sackcloth and ashes, mourning the wickedness and the terrible situation they were in, and Nehemiah said to the people 'Don't mourn! This is a time to rejoice!' John wanted everyone to rejoice and in all things give thanks. He shared how God had poured out his blessing on their two weeks of honeymoon, and explained why he had requested we sing the song 'We bring a sacrifice of praise into the house of the Lord'. As we sorrowed, it was a sacrifice of praise to remember who Gail was and what she had done in our lives. He didn't believe there was a single person present who had no reason to rejoice before God.

Someone had said 'Gail had two weddings in two weeks' and John felt really blessed to have been her husband for two weeks of laughter and joy. As they had prayed together John had felt frustrated that they could only understand God from the shadows, but now, he said, Gail saw Him face to face, feeling no pain, worshipping her Lord like we would never be able to while here on this earth. John desired that everyone be touched by the Holy Spirit and he prayed everyone would meditate on the good things each one had personally, and worship God, Creator, Lord and King, and give Him glory and honour for all the good things He gave us.

Con Heyns who took their wedding service spoke next, followed by Mike Oman who flew from Ireland within hours of hearing the news of Gail's death. Debbie and Anneke, Gail's co-workers shared, and then a tribute from the Pastors in Mozambique was translated from Portuguese. Part of it said:

> 'Since 1991 she worked with the church, teaching, preaching and counselling mothers; a work given by God.
>
> Gail worked much in the area of Manga. To develop her professional experiences she opened a school for pastors, teaching them English. To equip the leaders of the churches more, she would take responsibility for housing the teachers who came to give biblical training here in Mozambique. During the war, Gail went from door to door of the people living in the affected area of Manga, with the purpose of encouraging those living in that situation.
>
> In honour of her memory we send this message.
>
> Gail! Leaving a husband, parents, sisters, friends, pupils and other family, accepting death, and leaving your social, moral, and intellectual qualities, you will serve as an example to us and a vital guide in the field of education on the mission field and socially.
>
> The leaders and Christians of the church "The Body of Christ" promise to follow your example in every way.'

Rikki finished with a brief word, including the fact that he felt a bit put out that Gail had got to heaven before him!

Before the service John prayed that the angels would rejoice, and after the service someone came to Rikki and said during the praise and worship he had looked up to the rafters of the building and saw angels rejoicing there!

We didn't get as far as the refreshments because there were so many people wanting to speak to us. Gail's dear friend Viv, who could not come from her teaching post in England for the wedding, was there, and Jackie with husband Tom, whom Gail and John were planning to see the following week, while they were in Zimbabwe on holiday from the UK. YWAMers who came from Mozambique and Malawi. So many people. So much love. We deeply appreciated it all, especially the prayers which enfolded us with God's peace and strength.

We received a letter the following week which said:

> 'It's probably not usual to "thank people" for a funeral service, but I feel so strongly the need to tell you all what light you radiate, what a strong example you were yesterday and how beautifully you speak the truth in Christ.'

To God be all the glory!

John stayed with us for six weeks, and after spending the last two fasting and praying and seeking God's plan for him, he returned to Beira.

During the Praise and Worship in our Sunday morning service soon after John left, God clearly said to me 'Write Gail's story.' Nothing was further from my mind at the time, but John found some of her diaries in Beira, and we found more at home. Together with her letters I had kept over the years, I realised it was possible.

On 31st September we were again in Beira, to witness Debbie's wedding to Elias, in both a civil ceremony, and a Christian wedding service. On Monday, 3rd October Gail would have turned 29 years. John, Rikki and I, our friend Joan from YWAM Canada, and Wendy went to the same beach where Wendy took the engagement photographs, and John scattered Gail's ashes in the waves. I threw a spray of yellow orchids into the water, and we spent time in quiet reflection, tears flowing unchecked. As Rikki and I stood together with John in the waves we told him we did not hold him to Gail's memory, and we hoped he would marry again. He said 'That won't happen for a long time, if ever,' and then, after a pause, ' But I did so enjoy being married.'

We received over 400 letters and cards of sympathy from around the world, and several quoted John 12 verses 24 and 25 where Jesus says:

> *'Truly, I assure you, unless a grain of wheat drops into the earth and dies, it remains single, but if it dies, it produces a rich yield. The one who loves his life will lose it, but the one who hates his life in this world will preserve it to eternal life.'*

Verse 26 goes on:

> *'If anyone serves Me, let him follow Me: then where I am, there also will My servant be. If anyone serves Me, the Father will honour him.'*

That is how this book came to be called *A Grain of Wheat*.

A Child of Mine

by Edgar A. Guest

'I'll lend you for a little time a child of mine' **He** said.
'For you to love while she lives and mourn for when she's
dead. It may be for six or seven years, or twenty-two or
three, but will you, till I call her back, take care of her
for me?

She'll bring her charms to gladden you and should her
stay be brief, you'll have her lovely memories as solace
for your grief. I cannot promise she will stay, since all
from earth return, but there are lessons taught down
there I want this child to learn.

I've looked the wide world over in my search for teachers
true, and from the throngs that crowd life's land, I have
selected you. Now, will you give her all your love, nor
think the labour vain, nor hate me when I come to call to
take her back again?

I fancied that I heard them say, 'Dear Lord, Thy will be
done. For all the joy the child shall bring, the risk of grief
we'll run. We'll shelter her with tenderness, we'll love her
while we may, and for the happiness we've known forever
grateful stay.

But should the angels call for her much sooner than
we've planned, we'll brave the bitter grief that comes,
and try to understand.'

You are Love.
      If I abide in love,
            then I abide in You,
               and You abide
                  in me...
Thank you for the gift
     of love.
Help me to share it
          in small,
              everyday situations.

Help me not to be afraid
           to reach out
        to a hurting heart
    or to dance
        with a joyful spirit.
Help me to share,
       to live,
         to breathe,
           to just be....
             Your
               Love !!

Chapter 14

Much Fruit

Rikki has always said 'When I get to heaven, and the Lord asks me to give an account of my life, I want to have baskets and baskets of fruit to put before Him.' Gail had baskets and baskets of fruit; some of it you have already read about. Since her death there is more which we would like to share with you.

Angus, whom Gail had encouraged to play guitar in the early days of Greystone Park Fellowship services, and who took over the leadership of their school Christian Union when she left, leads one of the best praise and worship groups in Zimbabwe, and is an extremely effective full-time Youth Pastor.

Gail's friends Dorothy, in South Africa, and Karen, in Australia, parted on bad terms. On hearing the news of her death, each of them realised how unnecessary the break in their friendship had been, and how precious true friendship was, and their letters of apology to each other crossed in the post, bringing a beautiful healing and restoration.

Dellanie, in New Zealand, had been 'doing her own thing' for two years, when the news of Gail's death reached her. It shattered her, and made her realise

how far off course she had wandered, while Gail was hanging in there, going on with God's plans for her life. She wrote saying she had imagined Gail looking down at her from heaven yelling 'Go for it!' It did not take her long to get back on track.

The Service of Thanksgiving for Gail's life was the first service Margie had ever come to in our church, although her husband had been attending for some years. It was a life-changing experience. As people spoke she realised her life was a mess and her marriage a shadow of what it should be, because of things in her past which had never been dealt with. During the following week she asked us for help. It took time, but she is now free, her marriage is wonderful, her family relationships healing, and her face radiant. She has a personal relationship with the King of kings.

Dave, who wanted to get into Formula One motor racing in England, and drive for Jesus, was bitterly disappointed when it didn't work out the way he planned, and wandered in a spiritual desert for nine long years. Gail wrote a poem while they were both still in England:

'To Dave'

So you've reached the end of your rainbow
And you didn't find your pot of gold
Now you're tired and you're confused
You don't know which way to go.

Where has God been?
Couldn't He have given you a hand?
You were trying to do it all for Him
You just can't understand.

Is there no hope?
Was it all in vain?
Did you travel the lonely miles
To find it held no gain?
Has it been wasted time?

My son don't take your eyes off Me
My ways are higher
And much wiser too, you'll see
It's all under control.

It's all part of the plan
There's a roadway prepared ahead
Give me your hand
*   and take the next step with Me!*

Through Gail's friendship, he became a part of our family. Not long ago he lay on the carpet at the front of our church and said 'I've come home! It feels so good.'

Gail longed for the street kids to be exposed to as many good things as possible, and hoped one day to take some overseas. Klaus, from Denmark spent much time expanding the musical foundation Gail began with her guitar lessons, and took eight boys with him to Denmark in 1995 on a three week visit during which they gave a number of concerts. Two of these boys were offered scholarships to study in Denmark.

One of Gail's dreams was to see the Christian community in Beira supporting, sharing and caring for one another much more than it did. Some months after losing Gail, John shared with the people in the English evening service how he really felt, deep down inside, regardless of what people were seeing on the surface. His openness brought more unity, love and understanding to the whole group.

Friends sent gifts of money, in lieu of floral tributes, and in memory of Gail's outstanding work. We decided to put this money in trust for the future needs of the children Gail loved. Lino, one of the Beira skids had surgery to close a hole in his heart in Harare at the end of 1996 and the fund paid for some of the medical expenses.

A letter we received from Margaret Anne Mead in South Africa was special:

'My husband and I were fellow campers with Gail and John at Mana Pools, and I, and later my husband, strolled down to the river and met Gail on the same Sunday morning on which the accident occurred.

She was reading something, which I recognised as the YWAM Prayer Diary, and this indicated to me immediately that she was a Christian. She told me her name and a little of what she was doing in Beira with the street children. I was genuinely impressed. Here was a young woman at a time and in a setting like that, taking the time to pray for unreached people groups. The other people in the camp were involved in every other sort of activity, but she was spending time with the Lord, and concentrating on those who did not know Him. This kind of commitment to prayer and to her work really warmed my heart.

I had just finished reading a book by Loren Cunningham regarding the whole story of YWAM, which was most enlightening and I have a copy of that same YWAM Diary. I almost took it with me on holiday, but decided against it, as we were away for a whole month and therefore had a lot of luggage in the car. However, because of Gail's dedication, I felt challenged to be sure to use it when I got back. Even more now I realise that somebody needs to take her place and pray into those areas which concerned her, and I just wanted you to know that I have committed myself to doing just that – if you like in memory of somebody whom I knew for less than one day, but whose love for the Lord and for people impacted me more than I can say.'

The following is printed at the end of the Mana Pools section of a very beautiful new wild life photographic publication called *Wilderness Heritage* by Colin Mead, Margaret's husband:

> 'If I may, I would like to end this section on a sad note, with a dedication to the memory of Gail Wickes (née Decker) a beautiful young Christian lady whom we met at Mana Pools, and who was killed by a buffalo while honeymooning there. She will be sorely missed by her new husband, her family and friends ... and not least by the street children of Beira, Mozambique, whom she served so lovingly.'

In January 1996 I spent a week in Beira to see what had been happening in the eighteen months since Gail died. It was an exciting and encouraging week. Two classrooms for the pre-school project Gail, Pastor Bonga and Wendy had worked on were under construction, and Mai Bonga and other ladies in the church were now trained pre-school teachers. The day I visited the project Pastor Bonga had applied to purchase adjoining land so that food could be grown to feed the children. He had no money, equipment or seed for this and it was thrilling to be able to say: 'Gail's Memorial Fund will provide it all.'

Filipe Manuel Alfredo who took over as Headmaster of Escola Ré-om when Gail went to Canada shared his vision to build the school Gail had always dreamed of. He and his wife have completed their YWAM Discipleship Training School in Dondo, and continue part of the Beira team.

The school started with Grade One and now provides all grades covering elementary schooling. Children who graduated from Escola Ré-om have started Government high school studies. There is great enthusiasm for the Escola Ré-om Football team which is guaranteed to continue with 150+ students enrolled each year. Many more children have been reunited with their families and attend schools near to their homes, still supported by YWAM Beira.

Our Brazilian YWAM friend Neto, and Charlene, his South African wife, were amongst those who came for Gail's thanksgiving service, and spend time with us. Early in February, 1997, Neto died of malaria, in Mozambique. Charlene and John had a long talk together, a few days after Neto's funeral, and she said how, after Gail died, she could not understand how the family could minister, in joy, to people who came to grieve. 'These were the ones who just lost a loved one,' she said, 'How is it I went to encourage and help them, and they encouraged and helped me? But now I understand the grace of God, and now people come to mourn with me, and I am able to encourage them.' The Lord blessed their time together, and as John left her, he gave Charlene a hug goodbye and said 'I'm really happy for you' and then they looked at each other and laughed, knowing how crazy those words would sound to anyone who overheard. But they both understood the hope they had, and the mind-boggling grace of God. What else could they do but laugh and be glad?

Much fruit! Fruit has been mentioned several times throughout the book. We believe God wanted this book written so He could harvest even more fruit for His Kingdom. You can be part of that fruit.

You have read Gail's story – the mad, the sad and the glad – and know she lived her life for Jesus. If she could say anything to you she would say it's never too late to **'Go for it!'**

If you want to become a Christian, with your name written in the Lamb's book of life, and spend eternity with God in His heaven, there are three simple things you need to do.

1. You must be 'born again', so pray the following prayer thoughtfully and sincerely:

> Father, I know that I am a sinner, but when Jesus died on the cross at Calvary He took all my sins away. I want to be free of everything that I have done wrong. Please forgive me now. I ask You to come into my life and take control. I want to live for You from now on. Please fill me with Your Holy Spirit, so that I have the power and authority to resist the devil from dragging me back to my old life. Thank You that I am free. Amen.

2. Tell a 'born again' Christian what you have done
3. Read, Talk and Do

Start reading a modern translation of the Bible; begin with the Gospel of John, near the beginning of the New Testament; share with God day-to-day things, just as you would with your best friend – that is prayer – and join a church which is alive and moving with God.

Then you will be part of that fruit too.

If you are already a Christian, and you know God has spoken to you long ago, but you have allowed things to get in the way of responding to Him, it is never too late to pick it up and run with it – better late than never!

Are you frustrated? Feel bogged down with responsibilities and commitments when you would rather be doing something for God somewhere else? Nothing happens to a Christian outside His specific plan when you ask Him to be Lord of your life. He can and will use you.

In the world today we face many hard things, but we have a choice – to cling to tragedy, turning our eyes inwards and retiring from the world, or making each situation a triumph, an opportunity to reach out to others with deeper understanding, compassion and love.

God bless you – we look forward to spending eternity with you!

Meanwhile if you would like to receive regular news of YWAM Beira, pray for individual members of staff, or pupils, or support the work in any other way, please write to us, we would love to hear from you.

Rikki and Margaret Decker
4 Dart Road
Vainona, PO Borrowdale
Harare Zimbabwe

Telephone: (263) 14-882427

"Ask God to give you new songs"

See the birds in the sky
See them soar, watch them fly
Hear their songs float thru the air
Not a worry, not a care

God the Father, knows them all
He sees them when they fall

See the beauty all around
Trees planted firmly in the ground
Lilies in the field grow
White and pure like the snow

They are clothed from above
In God's beauty and His love

There are people everywhere
Some don't see
And some don't hear

They don't know He came to save
They don't know about the life He gave
We've got to show them
We've got to care
The love He gave us
We've got to share.

Postscript

John

Born on 3rd July, 1958 in Fort Worth, Texas, he was the youngest of five – two brothers and two sisters. He became a Christian when he was five, and dedicated his life to work for God at nine years old. From 1962 to 1969 his parents pastored a church in Salt Lake City, with a particular missionary outreach to the Mormons. His father, Homer, was killed in a car accident on 2nd August, 1969, and his older brother was killed in a plane crash on 2nd July, 1971. From 1973 to 1976 he lived in Bolivia where his mother, Betty, was a missionary nurse at the New Tribes Mission School. Between 1976 and 1980 John studied for a BA Psychology with a minor in Religion, and spent four months in Gaza, Israel. Between 1981 and 1982 he walked in a spiritual wilderness, working as a house builder, and in the Forest Service. The next year was spent in Jordan, working at a Baptist Hospital. Back in Salt Lake City, working again as a house builder he got back to church, to Bible study, became a church Deacon, then an Elder, and eventually pastored Calvary Chapel for three and a half years. He was particularly interested in working with street people, and making mission trips to Mexico.

In 1993 he joined Betty in Zimbabwe and both worked at the Sanyati Mission Hospital. He knew God clearly wanted him in Africa, but didn't know why. After six months he moved to Mozambique and worked with AIM – Africa Inland Mission. This job was completed just as he and Gail announced their engagement. Since Gail's death and his return to Mozambique, John has acquired a 15-year lease on 17 acres of land near Beira Airport, where he has established 'Kedesh' named after one of the Old Testament 'Cities of Refuge'. It is now fenced and relatively secure and electricity was connected early in 1997. Vocational training for older street kids began almost immediately, teaching animal husbandry and farming techniques as well as building, and carpentry skills. John is slowly introducing fruit and ornamental trees as well, and the plan is to be self-sufficient. Renovation of the derelict buildings is an ongoing process as funds permit.

In January, 1997, John agreed to do a YWAM Discipleship Training School in Harare, Zimbabwe, before officially joining YWAM leadership. At the end of this six month school he will spend two months with family and friends in the United States, before returning to Kedesh.